LEAVING
HOME

FAMILY LIVING
IN PASTORAL PERSPECTIVE

FAMILY LIVING IN PASTORAL PERSPECTIVE

LEAVING HOME

HERBERT ANDERSON
AND KENNETH R. MITCHELL

WESTMINSTER/JOHN KNOX PRESS
LOUISVILLE, KENTUCKY

Scripture quotations from the New Revised Standard Version of the Bible are copyright © 1989 by the Division of Christian Education of the National Council of the Churches of Christ in the U.S.A., and are used by permission.

Excerpts from "Little Gidding" in FOUR QUARTETS, copyright 1943 by T. S. Eliot and renewed 1971 by Esme Valerie Eliot, reprinted by permission of Harcourt Brace Jovanovich, Inc.

Book design by Drew Stevens

First edition

Published by Westminster/John Knox Press
Louisville, Kentucky

This book is printed on recycled acid-free paper that meets the American National Standards Institute Z39.48 standard. ∞

PRINTED IN THE UNITED STATES OF AMERICA
9 8 7 6 5 4 3 2 1

Library of Congress Cataloging-in-Publication Data

Anderson, Herbert, 1936–
    Leaving home / Herbert Anderson and Kenneth R. Mitchell. — 1st ed.
        p.   cm. — (Family living in pastoral perspective)
    Includes bibliographical references.
    ISBN 0-664-25127-7 (alk. paper)

    1. Family—Religious life.   2. Parenting—Religious aspects—
Christianity.   3. Autonomy in youth.   4. Parent and adult child.
5. Intergenerational relations.   I. Mitchell, Kenneth R.
II. Title.   III. Series: Anderson, Herbert, 1936–   Family living in
pastoral perspective.
BV4526.2.A525 1993
248.8'45—dc20   92-33115

This book is dedicated to Kenneth R. Mitchell (1930–1991),

who was for me a dear friend,

a thinking and writing partner,

a soulmate,

and probably the best crap detector one could ever expect to find.

Herbert Anderson

CONTENTS

INTRODUCTION

I DON'T REMEMBER when I first thought about leaving home as a religious task. It may have been when my mother was so disappointed that my first pastoral call would take me far away from her to California. It may have been one Christmas when I insisted that my family drive across Pennsylvania in freezing rain because it was still my job to rescue my mother from her depression. It may have been when I struggled to support candidates for pastoral ministry who believed that God had called them to serve within a 100-mile radius of Boxholm, Iowa. Or it may have been when my own children began to leave home, and I understood in a new way the importance of blessing our children as we send them out for their own unique journeys.

As the parent of children in their mid-twenties, I am keenly aware of the temptation to follow their lives in my dreams. Kahlil Gibran has an admonition for parents in *The Prophet* that is both necessary and difficult for us to hear. You can house their bodies, Gibran reminds parents, but not their souls, because "their souls dwell in a house of tomorrow you cannot visit, not even in your dreams."[1] It is the phrase "not even in your dreams" that is hard for me. I am eager to know of their plans for their future. I need to be reminded now and then that it is *their* future and not mine. The temptation is great not only because I love them but because their landscapes are not as limited as mine.

Both leaving and letting go have religious overtones because they relate to discovering the gifts each person has to give in the name of God and for the sake of the world. Because leaving and letting go are about home, we are also aware that making a home and regarding the earth as our home have become critical themes for our time. Family values and home making have become major political issues. And the Earth Summit that is being held in Brazil while I put the final touches on this manuscript has heightened our awareness of the threats to the galaxies and "this fragile earth, our island home."

The Aim of the Book

This is a book about leaving home, written for those who are leaving. Since leaving home is a lifelong process, material has been included here from many points along the journey. This book is for parents who celebrate a son or daughter's leaving *and* struggle to let him or her go graciously. It is also written for those who are professional helpers with people engaged in the complex and sometimes emotionally charged task of leaving home. The frame of reference is pastoral, but we believe that the book will be of benefit to anyone working with people on leaving home issues.

So much depends on leaving home well. The current popular literature about codependency is in part built on the assumption that patterns we established in our families of origin are likely to be repeated unless we choose intentionally to do things differently.[2] Doing things differently is one way of talking about leaving home. The multiplication of support groups for people struggling with codependency attests to the power of those patterns from our families and the power of the families themselves to resist our efforts to change.

We may be very gifted people, but if we cannot leave home, we are often not free enough to exercise those gifts in the fullest possible way. Because our first experience of intimacy in our family was confining, getting close to someone is a frightening thing. We have difficulty getting married and do not know why until we discover we have not yet left home. Or we may find that wherever we work or play, we end up in the same role of the responsible one that we had in our original family.

Leaving home is a significant part of the formation of a self. It is a natural aspect of maturing, and both the one who leaves and those who are left recognize that it is desirable and appropriate. Understanding the process, however, requires some care. Just what is the home that people leave? Are there some ways of leaving home that are better than others? When a young person does take the necessary step to leave home, why are families likely to establish impediments to accomplishing what they regard as a necessary developmental task? One aim of this book is to understand what is at stake in the complex ordinary process of leaving home. Another is to identify leaving home as a transition that marks out a critical task in the family's life cycle.

Looking at Family from a Life Cycle Perspective

In whatever society or group we exist, we are all individuals and at the same time members of a community. It is almost impossible to say whether membership or individuality has the greater power at any given time. We affect and are affected by the contexts in which we live. Membership in nation and tribe, in community and church, and most of all, in family has a profound effect upon every human being.

That particular, intimate, often conflicted crucible that is the family begins to shape us even before birth. Our families hand us a legacy—their sense of what is right and wrong, their rituals, their peculiar rules—all with the sense that these are not peculiar at all, but the universal rules by which human beings live. It is often a shock to discover that our family's "way" is only one of many ways, and that the way we thought was universal might not even be the best way. This legacy is nonetheless the best resource we have to negotiate the transitions and changes that mark out a family's history.

Families are always changing because individual members change as they grow up or grow older. The needs of the family as a whole also change as a consequence of changes in membership and circumstances. Some of those changes are anticipated, some are not. Like it or not, the family is not a fixed sum. The ability to adapt to change is therefore an essential characteristic of a family's capacity to move toward a future in which God is always making something new.

Throughout the life of any family, change is constantly taking place. Some changes are so minor as to have seemingly little impact on the family, while others are major events marked with strong emotions, and perhaps with some form of public celebration. This book is about those changes: recognizing them when we are going through them, caring about others when they are undergoing change in their family lives, and thinking about some of the profound issues that may be hidden in a particular change.

Sometimes, as with leaving home, even necessary changes are resisted. Families sometimes seek to establish stability by limiting change. Or they may attempt to establish continuity in the midst of change through customs, traditions, rituals, the naming of children, the preservation of heirlooms, the fostering of family myths. While continuity between a family's past and its future is a necessary thing, it sometimes comes at the expense of the freedom of individuals within a family to maximize their gifts.

It has been assumed for some time that individuals

change according to relatively predictable phases. Each phase is marked by a crisis that needs to be resolved in the interest of individual growth. Every individual life-cycle crisis is also a family crisis. Individual transitions into and out of different family relationships and roles—such as leaving home, getting married, becoming parents, coping with living alone—are interrelated with changes in the family as a system. And the family's capacity to change will create a context of freedom for individuals to grow.[3]

The family as a social system changes according to its own history of evolving tasks. Each major transition in its life cycle offers a family the possibility to become something new. Such moments of transition create a crisis in the ordinary sense of that word because they are turning points at which things will either get better or worse. It is not really possible to have change without crisis or without grief. A family's capacity to grieve its anticipated—as well as its unanticipated—losses will in large measure determine its ability to live through the crises of change.

This emphasis on the family's life cycle is the most practical and effective way of helping people understand the family as a social unit with a life and history of its own. It also provides a framework for thinking about how ordinary pastoral interventions related to the church's ritual life correspond to critical moments of transition in the family's history. The church's ministry with families often requires a delicate balance between attending to the needs of individuals in transition and the needs of the family as a whole.

This book is the first of a series. Each volume will examine one of the major changes that can be expected in the ordinary life cycle of a family. For every transition, there is frequently a significant event that initiates a new family task. As a family moves through its history, the tasks accumulate and then eventually are reduced, as Figure 1 suggests.

FIGURE 1

Transitions and Tasks in the Family Life Cycle

Transitional Event	Leaving home events	Wedding	Birth of first child	Last child leaves	Death of a spouse
Family Tasks	Leaving home	Becoming married	Raising children	Promising again	Living alone
	Identity formation	Leaving home	Becoming married	Raising children	Identity re-formation
		Identity formation	Leaving home	Leaving home	
			Identity formation		

Each of the volumes in this series will address one of the tasks of the family: leaving home, becoming married, raising children, promising again, and living alone. In the course of a family's life cycle, each of those tasks is initiated by a transitional event or events. Like every schema, this figure does not fully represent actual living. We are aware that there are many variations because people divorce and re-marry, because some people leave home and then live alone, and because some people marry but do not have children. For those people who marry and have children, however, these transitions and tasks mark relatively predictable changes over time that define a family's history.

Living in Families Means Living with Paradox

If change is central to the vitality of a family's life over time, paradox is what gives shape to its meaning and sustains its well-being in time. Paradox is defined in dictionaries as a "seeming contradiction," and some of the dictionaries point out that the seeming contradiction may in fact be real. Somehow, two things that cannot both be true are true, and those who experience them "in the flesh" are left to puzzle out what is really true. Paradox is in the order of things. Life involves continuity and discontinuity at the same time; the way to stay together successfully demands separation; people need to be loved as they are in order to be free to change. The task is not always to overcome paradox but to learn to live with it and in it. Maintaining equilibrium is not just preserving a negative status quo but a matter of keeping the paradox as well balanced as possible.

A troubled family does not or cannot notice change, and does not or cannot take steps to grieve losses and celebrate new gains. It is a major task for helpers of many kinds to help family members see change and to spend time and energy reconstructing a system that can undergo change. Similarly, the family that copes poorly with the paradoxes of existence is the family that resists the paradox by insisting on remaining on one side of it. The family that sticks to tradition—and so clings to continuity—will have a difficult time acknowledging change and may even threaten its own survival, and the family that is only open to discontinuity and newness loses a sense of its roots.

Paradox remains even when change occurs. Parker Palmer has expressed it well when he suggests that the deepest truths of life can only be expressed with paradox. "To allow one's life to be torn by contradiction and swallowed up in paradox is to live in the reality of the resurrection, in the sign of Jonah. . . . And the cross speaks of the greatest paradox of all—that to live we have to die."[4] The belief that paradox is the constant condition of human life understood in the light of God is a central motif of this book.

> A chair is mostly space
> But it is solid enough to sit in.
> A family is mostly space
> But it is solid enough to live in.

This verse conveys in a sprightly manner the idea that the family is always a paradoxical reality. It is both a civil institution and the church in miniature. It promotes community and honors individual autonomy. It is necessary to leave home in order to go home again. Or as dramatist Henrik Ibsen once observed: If you can't stand to be alone, don't get married. Families are likely to get in trouble when they do not keep alive both dimensions of the paradox. On the other hand, families remain vital if they can stay in the contradictions that finally only God can resolve.

If paradox is at the center of any theology of the family and central to its spiritual well-being, then our ministry with families may in fact require that we intensify the contradictions by saying the other side. It is our pastoral task to intend paradox precisely because the crossing point is the point of transformation. From a pastoral theological point of view, paradox is the constant condition of human life in the light of God.

Writing about change and paradox involves an effort to speak descriptively and normatively at the same time, and that, too, is paradoxical. It involves living with a vision of how a family ought to be, and with the vast differences in how families are. People behave in patterned but amazingly varied ways, and we need to understand both the patterns and the variations.

Intending paradox as we use it here is not the same as what family therapists refer to as *paradoxical intervention,* pushing families in one direction in the hope that they will end up moving in the other (desired) direction.[5] In such situations, paradox is a tool. We believe that paradox is not just a means, but an end and a normal state. The helper's task is to assist people to live in the paradoxes of existence.

Remembering Ken Mitchell

This series of books has had a lengthy period of incubation. Not long after Ken and I completed *All Our Losses, All Our Griefs,*[6] we began thinking about a publication on the family life cycle and pastoral ministry. At that time, we intended to amplify the schema of five epochs that I had developed in *The Family and Pastoral Care.*[7] Because of changes that occurred in our personal and professional lives, the process moved along at a snail's pace. In one sense, the slow pace was providential. The criticism that the model of five epochs was too artificial and disconnected from the way families live moved us instead in the direction of tasks and transitions. And the longer we thought together, the more we had to say. Quite spontaneously, during an airport lunch, we realized that if we were having difficulty writing one book, five would be easier.

We agreed that each volume would address the following: major tasks of the family throughout its history; rituals that enable effective transitions as those tasks change; beliefs and values from the Christian tradition that shape and are shaped by those family tasks; pastoral opportunities in response to those family life-cycle agendas.

Progress moved slowly until the summer of 1990 when I began a sabbatical supported by a grant from the Association of Theological Schools. During the fall we finalized the outlines for each of the five volumes and by Christmas, the present volume was completed with the exception of chapter 5, which Ken intended to draft. However, he had only begun to work on it when he died suddenly of a heart attack on February 18, 1991. Although I have done all of the rewriting since his untimely death, this volume remains a joint enterprise with Ken.

Subsequent volumes in this series, to be written with a variety of authors, will inevitably be different from what Ken and I had planned, even though the books will follow the outline that had been developed before Ken died. We will miss his skills at editing and writing. Ken had a way with words that is a rare gift. He is greatly missed.

Acknowledgments

I am very grateful for the encouragement from many quarters to continue this project and particularly for the support of Harold Twiss and Westminster/John Knox Press as I waffled about completing the series. I am also grateful to the friends (new and old) who have agreed to join with me in completing this adventure: *Becoming Married,* with R. Cotton Fite; *Raising Children,* with Susan B. W. Johnson; *Promising Again,* with David Hogue and Marie McCarthy, S.P.; and *Living Alone* with Freda Gardner. Their participation has enriched my thinking about family tasks and transitions in ways that are reflected in this first volume.

There are two other groups of people who deserve thanks,

one of whom can be named and the other cannot. A number of people have read portions of these chapters and offered valuable suggestions and timely criticism. They include R. Cotton Fite, Richard Jensen, Susan B. W. Johnson, Dale Ehrman, O.S.C., Marie McCarthy, S.P., Lawrence Rywalt, C.P., Doug Purnell, Carol Joncs Sherman, and Coleen Smith Slosberg. I am particularly grateful to Karen Speerstra who has offered editorial advice and personal encouragement without which this volume as it is would not have been possible.

Over the years students and participants in workshops have taught us about leaving home by telling their stories. Some of those used here have been disguised in order to be included in this volume. While their real names do not appear, these people who have shared their journeys from home have been internal conversation partners with me in the rewriting after Ken's death. I am grateful for their presence both in the book and in my remembrance. The stories ascribed to Kenneth and Herbert are, however, the actual stories of the authors.

Leaving home is seldom without difficulty. My hope is that those who read this volume will find something to make the transition easier for themselves or the people for whom they care.

HERBERT ANDERSON

Pentecost, 1992

1

STARTING
FROM HOME

MY FATHER'S first question on meeting one of my college friends was always the same: "Where's home for
you?" My friends usually named the place where their
parents lived. But when he kept asking that question for
some years after I left college, the answers became less predictable. Some of my friends thought he meant, "Where do
you live?" He didn't; he meant, "Where do your parents
live?" or "Where did you start from?" Those who grasped
that meaning responded appropriately, and made him happy.
He was annoyed by my friend John, who answered, "I make
my home here." To my father, home was not something one
made but something one had. Home was Muncie and only
Muncie, even after he had married and was rearing his own
children miles and miles away. At the age of twenty-six he
married my mother and moved to Cincinnati, but when he
said "home" he meant Muncie, Indiana—until his mother
died.   (Kenneth)

When someone asks Where's home for you? we might
think of the place where we spent our childhood or we might
have in mind the place where we now live. Both are correct.
Home is where we come from and where we live now. Home is
the places and the people from the past and in the present who
claim our allegiance and hold our affections.

Home is where the heart is. For Kenneth's father home was Muncie until his mother died. Our heart may be in the home of our childhood or where our parents still live or where we live now. It is the community that we keep close to ourselves wherever we are. We may have fond memories, sad memories, or bitter memories of home, but it is nevertheless the place and the gathering of people which, loved or hated, is built deeply into our personalities and our lives. Home may begin as a physical place but what endures is an emotional reality that transcends time and space. In that sense, we may leave home but home never leaves us.

This is a book about leaving home. It is about the process of separating emotionally from the home of our origin. That process happens over time. Most of the time, our energies are focused on the journey ahead: where we will live, with whom we will live, what we will do, when will our parents let go, and so on. Paradoxically, our freedom to return home is a sign that we have successfully left home. We may never live there again. We may visit the home of our origins very seldom. Even so we feel free to return without fear of losing who and what we have become since leaving. When we are able to claim it as the place of our beginnings, when we can in that sense go home again, then we will know we have left. And if we understand the home from which we came, it is likely that we will understand the journey from home more clearly.

Home: A Particular Place with Particular People

When we say home we usually have something very particular in mind. We mean this house on that street in such-and-such a town. A familiar skyline. Mist on the water in the morning. The stifling heat of summer. The barn we played in. The winter when the river froze over and dad drove his Plymouth across it. The whistle of the steam locomotive at bedtime. The word for home in any language evokes a multiplicity of images. And each one is quite particular.

The emotions stirred by remembering that place or those people we call home will also be particular. Long after the house has been torn down to make way for a freeway, long after the family has moved to a new and bigger house in a new town, we remember home as the place of warmth where cookies were baked and friends gathered or a painful place where a drunken father wreaked havoc. The places where we lived as children continue to evoke powerful emotions long after we have left them.

Home is a particular structure in which a family lives. Most adults can recall a favorite play spot or the place to hide when dad got mad or the always-dark room in the cellar or the room to which we were sent when we got too angry or too sad and violated the family's rules about permissible feelings. We remember the shape of a worn spot in the kitchen linoleum, empty liquor bottles in a closet, the smell of an elderly aunt's bedroom, the swing on the elm tree in the back yard.

These memories of the homes of our childhood are sacred. People who visit their childhood homes often wish they had let them remain, undisturbed in memory.

> The worst mistake I ever made was going back to see the house where I grew up. The beautiful oak stairway and majestic French doors had been painted a hideous brownish-orange with a glossy finish! My parents would turn over in their graves if they knew what happened to their magnificent Victorian mansion. (Marco)

Even if nothing has been changed, the house looks much smaller, the trees are not where we remember them, and the hill behind the house is a slight incline. Where we lived as children is what we remember.

Home is a company of people with particular values and

a particular history. Some of the memories of those particular groups of people bring immense comfort, deep longing, a kind of sadness when they are gone forever. Other memories are so painful we avoid them if we can. Or we may be grateful that we are no longer subjected to that nasty smell, those awful chores, the fears of unpredictable abuse, those cold nights in unheated rooms.

Memories we recall with ease, those we work to dredge up, and those so repressed that monumental effort would be needed to bring them to consciousness, all have the power to shape our lives and our personalities. We sometimes make choices based on recapturing or avoiding the repetition of an old experience.

> I could not stand the smell of lavender but I did not know why. It never really mattered to me until Jocelyn began to use lavender to make our bedroom smell good shortly after we were married. She thought my response was "out of proportion" and told me so. What she did not know (and what I could not tell her because I did not remember immediately) was that the stern grandmother who raised me perfumed her room with lavender. She died when I was five years old. I do not remember my grandmother but I do remember the smell of lavender. (Jamal)

In our childhood homes we learn to "dance a particular dance" the steps of which we fall into automatically, even when we have forgotten how, where, or why we learned them. Jamal did not remember his grandmother, but he remembered the smell and with it a host of expectations of how to behave "in the presence of a woman."

Home is where one starts from, T. S. Eliot said.[1] It is the particular womb out of which we are born. Because we are dependent for a long time on our families for nurture and care, it is not surprising that we have strong attachments to the places and people from which we "start." Home connotes roots. It is where old familiar tales are told that everyone understands. It is where we expect our needs will be met, even if they rarely or never have been. Whatever else it means, home is about origination, the places and people constituting our origins. When we lose those homes, the pain may go as deep as it did for Greg.

> Every item of farm machinery sold at the auction triggered memories of my childhood. It was as if people drove away with bits of my life. For my parents, it was worse. They had invested thirty years of their life together improving a farm that now the landlord was taking back. The story of their lives passed in review as the auctioneer sold off the machinery and livestock. When the last tractor had disappeared from sight and the sound of cows and hogs and sheep was silenced, I was overwhelmed with sadness. I had never really left the farm and now it had been taken from me. While I still cherished all the memories life on the farm had given me, I no longer had a place to which to return. I do not know how long the memories will last without a place to hold them.
>
> (Greg)

The Paradox of Being Home and Leaving Home

Although home is the place we start from, we usually do not stay there. We need to leave home in order to establish a way of living determined by our own decisions and hopes. We need to leave home in order to bring some conclusion to the formation of a separate self. We need to leave home in order to make a home of our own. And we also need to leave home so that we are free to go home again as adult individuals. Home is simply the place we start from.

Leaving home may include a physical separation, but it primarily involves an emotional differentiation from the family where we originated. It is usually the claims of the people we call family more than the place we call home that make it difficult for us to leave. Whether we stay near where we start from or put a great deal of physical distance between ourselves and our first home, the emotional task is the same. *Leaving home means a readiness, willingness, and ability to make one's own decisions, and to make one's way in the world without undue emotional dependence on the home one has come from. Leaving home also involves a change in status or role in one's family of origin that makes it possible for parents and children to be adults together.*

What we mean by leaving home is part of a larger process that begins when we are born and may still be going on when we are middle-aged and sometimes even after our parents have died. It is anticipated by significant events along the way: going alone to grandma's or camping out in the back yard or taking the bus to school or sleep-overs or going to camp or opening a checking account or traveling abroad. Later in life, leaving home could include the choice of an occupation, a decision about where to spend Christmas, or the selection of a car. While each of those moments may become a step toward the formation of a self, some steps are more formative than others. Our focus in this volume is on the period in individual and family life when the task of leaving home is a primary agenda for both the individual and the family. Leaving home in this specific sense usually occurs in late adolescence and early adulthood.

However, we cannot understand the necessity of leaving home unless we understand what it is to be at home. Being home and leaving home parallel the two great human longings for belonging and community on the one hand and autonomy and independent action on the other. This paradox of being home and leaving home is expressed in different ways throughout our lives. Leaving home presupposes that we have a home from which to begin and we leave that home so we can be at home where we subsequently live. This paradox of being home and leaving home parallels a more fundamentally paradoxical understanding of the family as a community of people who honor autonomy as they live together.

Balancing Home and Pilgrimage

In a sense, it was an arbitrary decision to begin this series of books on the family life cycle with leaving home rather than with becoming married. In another sense, however, beginning with leaving home is a logical continuation of the metaphors of "development" that have dominated this era. Words such as journey and pilgrimage and transformation, as well as various theories of change, have dominated the secular as well as the religious imagination. They are powerful metaphors, pointing us beyond ourselves to something new, something not yet fulfilled. But they are incomplete. We agree with Sharon Daloz Parks when she suggests that at this moment in history, the formation of adequate expressions of meaning and faith and perhaps the future of our planet home "is dependent, in part, upon the liberation, reappropriation, and renewed companionship of the metaphors of detachment and connection, pilgrims and homemakers, journeying and homesteading."[2]

Metaphors of development emphasize only one half of the fundamental human paradox of being separate together, of autonomy and community, of being home and leaving home. Homemaking and homesteading are part of the other half. The story of human development as journey, pilgrimage, or adventure cannot be separated from stories of home, dwelling, and communion. The journey always has a beginning. Since home is where we start from, leaving home needs the parallel image of being home in order to express in the fullest possible sense our personal and social experience of human life.

The emphasis on pilgrimage or journey is consistent with much of Christian teaching. Our origins in Hebrew history include stories of pilgrimage, wandering, exile. Christians have also used the pilgrim image frequently. Our journey on this earth is toward our true home with God. If the growth of a religion depends on transcending our attachment to place or homeland, then it is not surprising that pilgrimage or journey dominate our religious imagery.

Being faithful people of God may, however, require staying as well as going, homesteading as well as taking the adventure. To become a pilgrim, to take the journey to an unknown region, is a sacred calling. But it may also be, as Carol Ochs has observed, a distraction from the immediate, present time in which we can act.[3] The urge to go on a journey can prompt us to look elsewhere for what is already close at hand or avoid the sacrifices that we must make to create a home. The metaphors of pilgrimage continue to challenge us to expand the places we call home. However, metaphors like homemaking invite us to discover what is really there in the places where we feel truly at home.

In a society in which mobility is the norm, it is easy to overlook this need to be at home, to have roots. As she moved for the fourth time in her married life, Mary Pellauer compared moving to some of the nastier regions in Dante's hell.

> Simone Weil's comments from *The Need for Roots* have haunted me during the past few months. "To be rooted is perhaps the most important and least recognized need of the human soul." Saying good-byes and closing boxes pulled up my anchoring roots one by one. I understand very well the notion of a pilgrim people who believe that nowhere on this earth is truly home. After just having trucked all these goods about again, feeling a strong need for the orientation that home provides, frankly I am not much attracted to this image. Even Nelle Morton's phrase, "the journey is home," which ordinarily moves me so, feels too strenuous and dislocated right now. I'd like a breather, a leisurely set of decades to sink my roots well down, to grow slowly back into a cosmos, a living universe of meaning.[4]

Dorothy's quest for home in *The Wizard of Oz* is another illustration of this fundamental human longing that Mary Pellauer has articulated. What Dorothy learns is that home is not just a place "out there" to be found but an inner disposition that must be nourished. From one perspective, Dorothy's story is remarkable, not so much in finding home again as it is making the world home for herself and others. Oz is not a separate world from Kansas but her vision of what is possible in Kansas. This longing to be "at home" in the world is a religious impulse. And making the world a home is a sacred task that calls us to be faithful to the suffering and joy of ordinary life.[5]

The restoration of home, homesteading, and homemaking as necessary and effective images of human wholeness will require that we keep in clear perspective a paradoxical vision of being human. It will no longer do to talk of men taking adventures while women "keep the home fires burning." When men accept responsibility for making a home, women will be free to go on long journeys. Both making homes and going on pilgrimages transcend issues of male and female, youth and age. The young may make homes while the elderly go on pilgrimages, or vice versa. Parks is correct: whoever does it and however it is done, we need to regard homemaking and homesteading as "activities which can build a space where souls can thrive and dream—secure, protected, related, nourished, and whole. . . . Homemaking as we are exploring it here is a connective, creative act of the human imagination and a primary activity of Spirit."[6] Only a balance between images of home and pilgrimage, between being home and leaving home, will effect both societal and human transformation.

Being Home in an Epoch of Homelessness

There are powerful forces around the globe that undermine this universal longing and need for a place called home.

Rootlessness is a characteristic of modern life in almost every culture. The reality of homelessness for millions of people around the globe who have been uprooted from the places where they lived by war or greed or racial oppression casts a long shadow on our consideration of being home and leaving home. It is not easy to promote the image of home and home-making when millions around the globe are homeless.

Not all homeless live on the streets. In industrialized soci-eties, people in the professional middle class, whose economic and social status is based on education and skills rather than on the ownership of property and capital, are not likely to settle down if that might impede moving up. These upwardly mobile transients never think of any place as their home or as anyone else's. The social critic Wendell Berry has suggested that these up-scale transients have no local allegiances. In order to be able to desecrate, endanger, or destroy a place, after all, one must be able to leave it and to forget it. One must never think of any place as one's home. No place is as valuable as what it might be changed into or what might be taken out of it.[7] From this perspective, as long as mobility is presumed to be the way to prosperity, homemaking *must be* regarded as self-defeating.

Excessive mobility means that many children have grown to adulthood without having known a hometown. "Hometown-lessness," like most everything else in life, is a mixed bag of advantages and disadvantages. Someone whose family has moved eight times by her sixteenth birthday learns very early that social conventions are mostly arbitrary. Such knowledge fosters a sense of independence and a skepticism toward con-ventional wisdom. Not everyone survives hometownlessness emotionally, however. Attachments that are disrupted over and over again are eventually diluted. Because loneliness is less painful than always leaving the ones you love, some choose to stop making attachments at all. The absence of a stable place and dependable relationships one might call home is often the source of great pain among our youth.

There are people who have a place to live, even a hometown, but are emotionally homeless, cut off from the kinds of relationships and human interaction that makes a house a home. They live in loneliness and terror behind locked doors. They are the emotionally homeless who are trapped by violence coming from people whom they both love and fear. They are the aged, the physically handicapped, the poor, the chronically ill who may have a place to live but are still homeless. They are the children of divorce who, like Marvin in the following story, may have many shelters and plenty of closets but no place to call home.

We cannot leave what we have not had.

> We moved around a lot when I was growing up. The places where we lived were simple but nice. There was the security of a roof over my head and food on the table. But that security was often shaken by the instability of my parents' marriage. Even before they divorced, I had begun a search for a more secure place, a place I could call my emotional home. Ironically, it has been with my father that I have found a home after many years of being distant from him. He and his new wife have worked very hard at making me feel a part of their new home. The physical place is a factor, but what really feels like home is the relationship with my dad. I feel I am now better able to accept my dad's unconditional love for me in the ways he is able to give it. For the first time in my life I feel a sense of rootedness and permanence. Even though I know I will be moving a great deal in my life, I have a place I can call home. That place is with my dad. That is the home for which I have been searching since I was a child. It is only in feeling I have a home base that I can venture out into the unknown world as a priest in a religious order.   (Marvin)

Many forces work against the recovery of collective and personal experiences of homemaking and home. Homelessness in its many guises is a global crisis that casts a long shadow on the art of leaving home. Like Marvin, whose parents' divorce left him without an emotional home, there are legions of children who wish they had a home to leave. For others, images of home are contaminated by memories of violence and abuse. Being home is mostly an experience of terror, which must be escaped. Neither men nor women can afford to ignore the ways in which images of home have been used to oppress. In western societies in particular, the values of homemaking need to be liberated from excessive privatization so that being home does not become an extension of exaggerated individualism.[8]

These factors represent a formidable opposition to the universal impulse toward homemaking. The solution is not to recreate Norman Rockwell's pictures of home. Nor is the answer to be found in promoting the creation of well-stocked "cocoons," which will be "havens in a heartless world." The dilemma facing families today is a split between values of body, connection, stability, belonging, familiarity, and hospitality on the one side and the values of separation, cutting clean, openness to that which is strange or the search for the yet unknown on the other. This split is a disorder that threatens human life as we know it. The restoration of the image of home in our public imagination is not only a matter of justice; it is a matter of survival.

Human life, both in an individual and in a communal sense, is sustained and enriched by venturing *and* abiding, separating *and* connecting. "We have learned much about the transforming power of pilgrimage. We need also to recover the transforming power of the art of home-making. The soul's discipline is shaped by both venturing and by abiding."[9] We are compelled to find ways to dwell together, to enlarge the boundaries of "home" so as to embrace our earth, to meet new relatives, and to practice the arts of hospitality. Therefore we believe that consideration of the task of leaving home cannot be separated from the task of making a home.

Characteristics of Home

Since home is always a particular place or people that evoke particular memories, images of home are richly varied. Some are filled with the pain of the abuse and violence that oc curred there. Other images are nostalgic because the actual people and places in our memories are hidden or vague. Still others are rich with stories, traditions, unforgettable characters, and memorable events. Some images of home may be so ambiguous that our efforts to make a new home are stymied. Yet for all this diversity, home has some common characteristics. If we can understand what it means to "be home," we will understand more clearly the process of leaving home. The marks of leaving home are shaped by what we regard as the characteristics of home.

A home involves a defined physical space. It is of course a place. But a house or place is not a home until the physical space has been transformed by symbols that identify and sustain a family as a particular human community. A friend of ours whose family was imprisoned in Indonesia by the Japanese during World War II remembers clearly his mother's capacity to make a home wherever they were. She had one or two valued objects that she used ingeniously to mark out the boundaries of home. She would then fill that limited, arbitrary space with stories and songs and rituals. She could make a home, even in an alien land, even under hostile circumstances.

Home is a defined physical space in which we live. It is living that makes the difference. Designer draperies ordered from an interior decorator to match the new carpet may add elegance, but they do not make a home.

When we went house-hunting twenty years ago, my husband Jack and I came across a home in our price range that seemed an incredible find. It was a large and stately brick colonial with carefully manicured grounds, and a sunken tub in the master bedroom, where French doors opened onto a handsome deck. Downstairs a massive fireplace dominated a paneled living room. The sun-room needed a total overhaul, but even so, the house proclaimed quality, elegance, and expensive good taste. We didn't buy it. I couldn't picture myself living there.[10]

What makes a house a home is a very subjective thing. Once the kitchen is in order or the books are on shelves or the curtains have been hung or the Christmas ornaments have been arranged on the tree at least once, then people will say that "It's beginning to feel like home." When that transformation does not happen, we may refer to it as "our place," rather than "our home." But when the physical space in which we live fits with who we are, a home has come into being.

In her book *The Journey Is Home,* Nelle Morton has described the painful struggle of women to find new definitions for themselves beyond "keeping the hearth." Breaking cultural expectations of where and who women should be has often been perceived as betrayal. Despite nostalgic longing to return home, women found that home had become a movement and a quality of relationships. "From the time I experienced myself as a woman and a stranger in a strange land or in exodus toward new time and new space, I came to know home was not a place."[11] The journey had become home. And that journey had begun at one's first home because the end reveals the beginning.

Home is a place of safety. It is a shelter, not only against the elements and from injury, but from terror and doubt. It is a context that protects those most vulnerable—our children and our elderly. To be home is to be safe. Home is where we expect our needs will be met, where we expect to be taken care of, where we will be able to let down our guard and allow the more childlike or childish side of our personality to emerge. If I am hungry, I will be fed. If I am sick, I will be taken care of. If I am weary, there will be space and freedom to rest. In a later volume in this series we consider the task of raising children; there we will explore more fully how the family needs to maintain a flexible balance between protection and freedom. Unfortunately, too many homes are no longer a place of safety. If home is not safe, then we are not only vulnerable, we are violated in the very place where we should be protected.

> When I was very young, I loved to make tents with blankets and chairs. I always felt safe when I was under cover. I used to imagine that the sky was a bowl upended over this planet. My parents gave me lots of freedom as long as I was "home before dark." As I grew older, I came to realize slowly that there was no "upended bowl" confining the atmosphere; when one looked upward, it was into infinity. I had a new appreciation of my parents' admonition to be home before dark. In daylight, infinity is inconceivable; at night, it is terrifying. I wanted a roof between me and the sky; to be without a shelter was to be naked in every possible way. Home is having a roof over my head. (Melissa)

The image of home as a place of safety has increased in significance as the world outside has become more dangerous. For Melissa, home was a roof against the terrors of infinity. We like to believe that home is a castle or fortress, safe from the world even though television makes it easy to penetrate. The interest in "cocooning" is prompted by the longing to create a home relatively insulated from the outside. However, even if a home is able to shut out influences from the wider society, it still may not be a safe place for some members of the family.

The idea of home as a place of safety is cruelly undermined in certain families. Self-esteem is damaged or never nurtured. The safety of women and children is too frequently in jeopardy in families today. At one time, our society operated with values that suggested that it was permissible (sometimes even advisable!) to inflict such damage upon children or women. Though our present society has begun to recognize the horror of such a stance, violence and abuse in the family has not diminished.

These dangerous homes, however, often have just as much emotional pull as would a safe place; they are still home. A setting that is not safe will still be home to a child growing up in that setting, and its pull may be powerful—so powerful that the child will resist and resent attempts to provide a safer environment. Dependent on a dangerous family for physical and emotional needs, the child often develops fear and love toward those people.

Home is where we belong. Home is something for which we feel we have some kind of proprietary right. In Robert Frost's "The Death of the Hired Man," the farmer Warren says that "Home is the place where, when you have to go there, they have to take you in."[12] The hired man who has lived on the farm property from time to time is visiting the family once again. He talks vaguely of working for them in the coming season. Yet there is no question in the reader's mind (or in the mind of the poem's characters) that the hired man has come home to die. He and they share the sense that he has a right to be there. It is where he belongs.

The longing to belong somewhere is universal. It is a very painful experience not to feel at home in the family of our origin. It can lead to a lifelong search for a lost parent or parents, or to a marriage in order to have "the family we never had." Sometimes this feeling prompts us to expect to be "taken in" by whatever people or place we have decided to make home. Maureen had a disastrous experience projecting her longing for "mommy and a daddy to love and accept me" shortly before she had this daydream.

I can't remember what I was thinking about when suddenly I seemed to see a bedraggled seven-year-old girl, sniveling and crying, bitching and scared, who kept tugging on grownups' arms, asking to go home with them. And one after another, they turned away or refused. And I thought, That's terrible, somebody has to take her in. Suddenly I recognized the child's face, and it was my own. And I remembered that when I was about seven and my mom was really angry with me, she said something that I heard as, "Well, you know we can always send you back where you came from." (Meaning the adoption agency from which in fact I did come.) And I remembered how scared I was that I might get thrown out of the house if I screwed up. And I thought, this poor kid's been crying for a home, a secure place where she'll belong no matter what. . . . And I thought about Jesus' words about how in his Father's house there were many rooms and he was going to prepare a place for us. If it weren't so, he would have told us, and I had a good cry. I was home, I would always be home, and so I could finally leave home, could finally give up clinging to a fantasy home.   (Maureen)

Home is a gift that we never earn. In the Frost poem, farmer Warren's wife offers a vision of home slightly different from her husband's. "I should have said it's something you somehow haven't to deserve,"[13] At its best, home is a place of grace because our acceptance is not conditional. One belongs by virtue of one's very existence. Unfortunately, not all families embody this conviction. Acceptance or love is conditioned on success or good behavior or fulfilling the perverse expectations of an abusing parent. When we get it right, however, we understand that each child is a gift for the family, and the home that is created to welcome and nurture each family member is a gift for the child.

Even though home is a gift we cannot—and need not—earn, it is a demanding place. Rules are necessary for the orderly functioning of a household. Individual needs have to be set aside for the sake of the family as a whole. Depending upon the roles members have in the system, they may be expected to earn money, provide food, care for children, maintain the space the system uses, perform chores, and fulfill other tasks necessary to maintain a home. The allocation of those tasks is delicate, and can become an occasion for oppression. When families function best, everybody is expected to fulfill specific responsibilities unless they are very young, very old, or very ill.

When we say that we do not feel at home someplace, it may be in spite of being welcomed and accepted. We often mean something about fit and familiarity. The smells are not the same. The ordinary sounds are different. The routines are strange. To be home is to be able to breathe more easily. That statement may be taken literally as well as symbolically; being in an unfamiliar place may make breathing so labored that a person becomes sick. When we are away from home we miss the familiarity that is like a womb: an environment so connected to who we are that we cannot imagine living outside it for long.

Being at home with God transforms all other experiences of home. It conveys a certainty of belonging that transcends human fickleness and conditional acceptance. It is the assurance of a peace and shelter that cannot be violated. Being at home with God is a promise that is the horizon for every present, fragmentary, finite experience of home. Garrison Keillor tells a story about having a "storm home" in his youth. Students were assigned a storm home in town when they started high school so that they would have some place to go if a snow storm prevented the buses from running. It never stormed during the week the entire time he was there. But he was always glad for the Krugers', his storm home. He imagined how they would welcome him, how delighted they would be to see him—and he was sustained by that promise.

The eschatological promise of being at home with God is like Keillor's vision of a storm home. It is like Maureen's daydream about the house with many rooms Jesus is preparing for us. The climax of God's mysterious design for humankind is a universal "homecoming" in which we abide forever in "a building from God, a house not made with hands, eternal in the heavens" (2 Cor. 5:1). In the meantime, we live in the promise that those who are led by the Spirit of God already have a place with God. This assurance that we are always with God enriches our ordinary, imperfect experience of being home and may even diminish our fear of leaving home. There is always at least a hint, and sometimes more than a hint, that the home each of us talks about is actually an echo or a pale reflection of a home with God that was the starting point for our pilgrimage and also its goal.

Home Is Where We Start From

These images of home are reflected in our experience of leaving. If home is understood primarily as physical space, then leaving home is a cumbersome process because a great collection of material objects "need" to be taken along to enable us to endure the strangeness of not being at home. Others can leave with less because they carry home within them wherever they go. Some people have difficulty feeling that they belong anywhere except at home. Those who experience homesickness are so in tune with belonging at home that being someplace else is physically painful and emotionally intolerable. Others are "at home" in the world, wherever they are. This ability to make a home may be the most important thing we take from our origins.

When we suggest with Eliot that "home is where we start from," we imply the ability to find new and creative ways to satisfy the emotional or physical or financial sustenance we received in the network of relationships and familiar places we have called home. There are other, more subtle implications: that home will go on being there after we have left; that if we get off to a false start we can go back home and begin again; that there is a place where we belong, a group that will receive us. We also mean that we could not leave these things behind if we had not had them in the first place. If home is where we start from, it does matter that we get a good start.

Leaving home is the logical extension of the formation of a self that begins at birth. The next chapter addresses the relationship between the task of leaving home and the lifelong process of forming a self. It is possible to be a self without leaving home, but the expression of that self will be limited. We need to leave home in order to become a person in the fullest possible sense.

Leaving home is necessary if one intends to form a new family. In the second volume of this series, we will examine in detail the relationship between leaving home and becoming married. We believe that the biblical mandate is correct: you must leave before you can cleave. The capacity for each spouse to bond or "join the marriage" is enhanced by clear boundaries between the new couple and their families of origin. "Getting divorced" from one's parents is necessary in order to become married.

Leaving home is a religious act. It is necessary that we be sufficiently separate selves to follow the call of God without confining ties to our family of origin. The family is a necessary institution in our society, but it cannot have the final claim on our lives. We will return to this theme of leaving home as a religious act in the final chapter of this volume.

Leaving home is necessary so that we can go home again. It is the freedom from the emotional claims of our families of origin that makes it easier to return, even for a visit. Adult sons and daughters are able to declare their own ideas and insist on their own decisions though parents seldom stop wanting to exercise influence, even after their children are in middle years. The family as a human system is reluctant to relinquish the roles it has assigned to its members. Grown children who cannot resist returning to those old roles when they are in their parents' home often find excuses not to go home again. If it is difficult for adult sons and daughters to return home, that is usually because they never truly left. In order to have a home and be at home, we have to leave home. And when we have left, we can go home again to visit or even to live without fear of giving up who and what we have become.

Sometimes people need to leave home in order to survive. In situations of emotional or sexual abuse, a child may grow up in such a distorted way that his or her personality is marked or cramped by childhood experience. There are also some homes in which physical abuse is so great that it threatens an individual's very survival. Leaving such a home is not merely a developmental task to be pursued at a particular time in one's life, but an utter necessity, one that may have to be faced long before a person is developmentally ready to make the move as an independent act.

We suspect that children leaving homes that are unsafe for them—emotionally, sexually, and physically—carry with them either a distorted image of home life, which then is transferred to future generations, or a gap, a hole, a nothing place where something should normally be found. We further suspect that those who must leave home before they are developmentally ready never really leave home, and thus as adults have a much harder time making a home.

To a large extent, we describe ideas about how families might be, but we also try to set them alongside descriptions of the way families are. Home, as we have been describing it, is in some ways an ideal. Many families in which children grow up

41

in our society are far from the environment we wish children to have. One of the difficult ironies we face in this chapter is that a place of that kind is still usually called home by those who grew up in it.

Procession and Return

To be home, to leave home, and then to return again are human expressions of a deeper religious pattern sometimes referred to as "procession and return." This idea that all things proceed from and return to the same source has been widely used in religious literature. The Bible as a whole starts with creation proceeding from God and ends with the final restoration of all things in God. Systematic theological reflection often begins with God as the origin of all things, continues with the procession of good creatures from God's creativity, and ends with the restoration of creation in Christ.[14]

The image of procession and return is reflected in the rhythms of nature and the expressions of God.

> For as the rain and the snow come down from heaven,
> and do not return there until they have watered the earth,
> making it bring forth and sprout,
> giving seed to the sower and bread to the eater,
> so shall my word be that goes out from my mouth;
> it shall not return to me empty,
> but it shall accomplish that which I purpose,
> and succeed in the thing for which I sent it.
>
> (Isa. 55:10–11)

This pattern of procession and return is also reflected in biblical stories and stories of faith from the Christian tradition. The prodigal son story is one instance. He was at home, left for the far country, and eventually returned to a tumultuous welcome. Augustine, the bishop of Hippo in the fifth century, used the prodigal story in his *Confessions* to describe his own movement away from God, the church, his mother, and his native Africa and then his return to them all as led by God. The gospel writers also use this image to tell about the life of Christ. "I came from the Father and have come into the world; again, I am leaving the world and I am going to the Father" (John 16:28).

The same theme of procession and return is made in a much different way in the last two volumes of C. S. Lewis's seven volume *Chronicles of Narnia*. [15] In *The Magician's Nephew,* creation is depicted as taking place by means of a single voice, singing in the darkness and through that singing, calling worlds into being. As the singing progresses, living organisms spring up: plant life first, then lower animals, and finally animals capable of self-awareness. The singing is so charged with power that even an inanimate object, a lamp-post, grows out of the remnants of an old one. In *The Last Battle,* this same world comes to an end, and all the characters we have met in the seven volumes are seen returning to their source: the Lion whose singing brought the world into being.

We believe that this framework of procession and return is a paradigm for all human ways of being and for living in families. T. S. Eliot makes a similar point in "Little Gidding" when he observes that "The end is where we start from." The beginning is often the end, and to make an end is to make a beginning. So home is where we start from. And it is what we return to in an emotional sense. But it is always different when we return. If it is not, we at least see it with fresh eyes because we have changed. When we are able to look at our origins in a new way, we can say we have left home.

> With the drawing of this Love and the voice of this calling
> We shall not cease from exploration
> And the end of all our exploring
> Will be to arrive where we started
> And know the place for the first time. [16]

Procession and return are mirror images of pilgrimage and home. Leaving home begins with being at home, and the end of leaving home is to be free to return to the home of our origins. And when we return we know our home "for the first time." It is the end and it is the beginning. If we are free to return, we are free to leave again. And if we can leave, we are more likely to return to see more clearly the place and community of our origins. With this paradox in mind, we turn now to consider the lifelong process of forming a self which includes, as one central moment or task, leaving home.

2

FORMING A SELF
AND LEAVING HOME

LEAVING HOME is both a specific moment in an individual's history and a process that happens over time. When people tell stories about leaving home, they often have a particular moment in mind. It happened when they got an apartment across town or left for college or joined the military or moved to another part of the world or began a permanent job (known to parents as "gainful employment"), while continuing to live at home. However, in some cultures, it is still expected that children not leave home unless and until they marry.

The leaving home moment is an individual decision that signals a new emotional separation from one's originating family. This specific change in how one lives or works or decides does not complete the emotional process of separation nor does it effect a shift in role status in the family automatically. It does indicate, however, that leaving home is an agenda not only for the daughter or son but also for the entire family.

Leaving home is also a process that happens over time. It is unlikely that one action of physical separation or one autonomous decision will sever the emotional bond between children and parents or establish a new status in one's originating family. The change in status in a family is not easily effected because it presumes a corresponding shift in authority, responsibility, and accountability that is frequently resisted. If the emotional ties to one's family of origin are particularly strong, there are likely to be many leaving home moments, and the process is often not completed until later in life.

> I was taught that the only cars worth having were those made by Ford. I knew it would offend my father when I bought another make of car and I was correct. He was offended. I was already in my early thirties before I bought my first non-Ford automobile. The decision not to buy a Ford was the first time I remember making a public choice that challenged my father's influence in my life. It was, I told my father, only a "second car." It remained the second car until some time later. After my father died, I stopped buying Fords altogether. (Cedric)

Cedric's observations about buying a Ford automobile contrary to his father's judgment illustrates both that the process of leaving home is often initiated by seemingly ordinary decisions and that it takes time to leave home. Making the Ford a second car was another major leaving home decision for Cedric. It is important for us to keep in mind that the process of leaving home may require many emotionally charged moments or decisions.

The Mutuality of Forming an Identity and Leaving Home

In a sense, leaving home is a metaphor for finishing the developmental tasks of childhood and adolescence. It is an action that presupposes enough self-identity so that initiative is possible. No one can leave home for us. By the time a child comes to the task of leaving home, the emerging self is well enough formed to undertake the kind of action that will demonstrate and even effect a new freedom in relation to one's family.

At the same time, those steps to leave home, however tentative, enhance the process of self-definition. Psychological separation both precedes a specific leaving home event and is facilitated by it.

For the adolescent and the adolescent's originating family, the primary task is the formation of a self with a clear identity. Leaving home is a secondary agenda. Once an event has occurred that puts leaving home on the family's agenda, the focus shifts and the impending separation becomes the primary task for the entire family. The continuing formation of identity depends on this differentiating action. The relationship between identity formation and leaving home is pictured in Figure 2.

FIGURE 2

Leaving Home Events

	Adolescence	Young adulthood
Primary	Identity formation	Leaving home
Secondary	Leaving home	Identity formation

The process of leaving home is most frequently inaugurated by an individual's physical departure from home. That departure may be temporary or permanent. It may be sudden or gradual. It may be open or secret. As we will observe in the next chapter, there are many ways to leave home. Some are clearly more effective and beneficial than others. Even though leaving home is a process happening over time, the physical act of leaving or the emotional trauma of deciding marks a crucial moment in that process, intensifies identity development that has already begun, and puts leaving home at the center of the agenda for the leaver and the family staying behind. Our intent in this chapter is to locate this process of leaving home within the larger framework of individual development within a family's life cycle.

Forming a self is not merely an individual event; it is a systemic one as well. The histories of the family and of the individual are inextricably linked together from the beginning. Family therapists have added an emphasis on the intimate connection between the emerging self and its significant systemic context to traditional individualistic approaches of identity formation. In the sequence of family tasks, however, the formation of an identity through adolescence comes first; it is followed by the differentiation of that self from family of origin.

Jay Haley has observed how the adolescent/parent separation process is likely to disrupt a family's stability and how the family's instability will undermine the necessary task of leaving home.[1] This mutuality of adolescent disturbance and family pathology illustrates the close linkage between self and system. If the family is in trouble or if the parents' marriage is in jeopardy or if one parent is in a personal crisis, the adolescent's steps to autonomy are likely to be impeded. A child's leaving home requires a reorganization of the family; family members will need to communicate in new ways and get their needs met differently.

Even the families that function best are destabilized by the struggles of adolescence. There is an inevitable emotional chaos that accompanies the adolescent's declaration of freedom. No one knows quite what to expect next except more chaos. Playing their role, parents continue to protect and adolescent children continue to insist on their freedom. It is a conflict that can be negotiated but not avoided. The family is giving birth to an adult; there is danger in that process, but there is also life.

Others have expanded the same theme. The German family therapist Helm Stierlin's work on separating parents and children has identified ways in which a negative family context may indeed disrupt inevitable and necessary dynamics of this individuating process. He linked problems of children's leaving home with a crisis in the lives of their middle-aged parents.[2] At a time when an adolescent's future seems free and without limits, middle-aged parents are beginning to discover their own horizons cluttered and increasingly finite. Whereas some parents want their children to go off and realize the dreams they never managed to accomplish themselves, others are reluctant to grant their offspring freedom to seek fulfillment and, quite possibly, surpass their own achievements.

Leaving home is a continuation of the process of separation/individuation that parents and children have been working on since birth. Although the adolescent child is anticipating leaving home by insisting on more and more freedom and autonomy and less and less parental control, he or she is still principally at work on identity formation. When it goes well, the process of leaving home solidifies and enhances the leaver's sense of self. It symbolizes the end of childhood for the individual leaving, initiates a major reorganization of the family as a whole, and inaugurates a more adult-adult relationship between parents and children.

Separateness and Togetherness:
The Paradox of Humanness

Human life begins in the life-giving union with a mother, a physical connection that is replaced by a social bond with the mother and/or other nurturing persons. Those bonds form the crucible out of which emerges what we call a "self." In the formation of a self, this original attachment is altered, but the bonds are never fully dissolved. Even if the early bond is broken prematurely, the need for attachment remains. Human beings are inevitably communal creatures who come to know life and to be selves within a matrix of significant attachments. Thus, leaving home begins with being home in the sense of this original familial bond. But we do not stay. We leave home in order to become a fully separate self. Home is one of the many things we must give up, as Judith Viorst has reminded us, in order to grow up.[3] And one of the reasons we leave home is to make a home that others eventually will leave.

This paradox of separateness and togetherness is not only essential for the development of a self; it is the foundation for effective family living. The paradox shows up at transitional moments in a family's life cycle and in the everyday tasks of family living as well as at critical individual developmental crises. Both individuals and families must make difficult choices on behalf of separateness and togetherness. Families are likely to get into difficulty if they stress one side of the paradox to the exclusion of the other. Being together and being separate are equally essential for the development of full humanness and the maintenance of viable human communities like the family.[4]

> I raised Jeff to become independent, but when he chose independence I found myself not ready to accept it. I was not aware how close we were as a family until Jeff left for college. There were many nights I went to bed but could not sleep. The family seemed incomplete without him. By his junior year in college, I thought I was coping with the separation until I found Jeff's beautiful collie, dead in our garage. It was like going through it all again. The dog was the last symbol of Jeff's presence. When I walked the dog, it was as if I had a little of Jeff still with me. That was always comforting. It seemed with the death of the dog that Jeff's separation from us was more complete.   (Michael)

Families often discover, as Michael did, how closely attached they are when someone leaves. Attachment is assumed or is so covert that it cannot be considered openly. When fami-

50

lies are open about attachments and equally open about the sadness of separation, leaving home may be difficult but it will happen without excessive anxiety or anger or guilt. If, however, the family is the sole source of attachment, then leaving home may evoke the kind of inconsolable grief that Michael felt.

The family is the principal emotional context in which our unique gifts are nurtured and autonomy is honored. It is the environment that fosters self-esteem and a wide range of cognitive and relational abilities. The freedom to differ, the ability to value one's individual worth and one's own unique thoughts, feelings, wishes, and fantasies are values respecting human autonomy that are usually learned first in the family. The development of full humanness within any community requires a delicate balance between separateness and togetherness. Being home and leaving home are therefore reciprocally connected.

Our growth into separate and distinct persons depends on a significant emotional attachment to people in the family in which we are nurtured and from which we must eventually separate. Personhood presupposes community. We may have grown up in a wide variety of communities, we may be male or female, we may differ in ethnic background, but we all had to begin in a small human community, a family. Some of those families had two parents, some were three-generation families, some were single-parent families, and some may even have been cottages with hired "parents" in a large child-care institution. If for any reason that emotional attachment is not present in any of those familial contexts, or is compromised at the beginning, individuation becomes more complex.

Every time a family takes up a new task in its life history, it has an opportunity to strengthen its existence as a community in which emotional commitment is possible. The attachment of a marital pair is the end of the process that we will call "becoming married." In the second volume of this series, we will focus on the process of cleaving or bonding that is made possible by successfully leaving home. Similarly, in the third volume we will examine how the bonding of the marital pair creates an environment in which a child's need for attachment and the freedom to separate are maintained. We are reminded again that "the end is where we start from." The tools we need for forming relationships and building community are first discovered in our families of origin.

We have emphasized attachment and the communal aspect of family living in an effort to balance the emphasis on individuation and leaving home. Attachments within a stable, nurturing environment are obviously not the only factors in the formation of a self. Each of us brings something unique to the world. The capacity to endure serious loss or deprivation in infancy is often attributed to something intangible that is often referred to as "temperament": that "something intangible" that is born in us. However, the promise of adaptability does not permit us to discount the responsibility of providing a nurturing environment for children. Theories of attachment have convinced us that we must put the need for stable relationships at the center of our understanding of how a self is formed and sustained within families.

Principles of Human Development and Leaving Home

There are widely differing theories of individual development that have emerged since the rise of dynamic psychologies. It is not our intent to rehearse all those theories, nor is it possible to establish which theories are more or less compatible with a family systems perspective of the formation of a self. We propose rather to identify some principles common to theories of human development and identity formation in order to locate the process of leaving home within this larger framework.

We are all agents in the process of our own development. The extent to which a particular theory allows for each individual's active participation in his or her own development varies considerably, but in every theory the person is a participant in the process, not merely a passive "receiver." We are not merely acted upon, but actors who shape how the self is formed. Our responses to the environment—physical and interpersonal—affect others in their behavior toward us. The differences among children in a family illustrate how each individual's idiosyncratic response to the same situation nudges their character down a different path.

Leaving home requires our action. It is not something anyone else can do for us. Parents may push their children out of the nest when it is time to go, but that is not leaving home. Being evicted is not the same as deciding it is time to move on. The capacity to decide or to act to bring oneself closer to an intended goal is a necessary part of leaving home. When we suggest in chapter 6 that leaving home is a religious act, we will explore how our personal action serves the goal of vocation.

> My father and mother are separated. I suppose that may be one of the reasons why my mother did not want me to go away to college. My older brother stayed at home and went to a local junior college and my mother expected me to do the same. I was so furious at the blocks she put in my way, I asked my counselor to talk with her. She visited with my mom when I was not there. After the counselor's visit, my mother never again spoke of her objections to my leaving home. The price I paid for leaving when I did was that mom never came to visit me while I was in college.   (Jerome)

In chapter 5 we will consider the helper's role of advocacy in the process of leaving home. In Jerome's situation, it is likely that the counselor's advocacy took over some of the work that Jerome needed to do himself in order to leave home. Families that push their children out when the children are reluctant to leave may unwittingly undermine the action of a daughter or son that is required to effect the kind of emotional separation required for leaving home.

The human process of growth from birth to death requires that we negotiate specific crises along the way. Some of these crises can be expected; others cannot. Erik Erikson has argued that the process of identity formation takes place within significant communities and that those communities are changed by the processes of individual development taking place within them.[5] When the community facing such change is a family, a crisis ordinarily occurs. Leaving home is a time of increased vulnerability and heightened potential for everyone.

Leaving home is a crisis both for the individual and for the family. The person getting ready to leave may precipitate a crisis by challenging familial expectations or standard procedures in an attempt to widen the range of autonomous action. This crisis is not unlike an earlier time in the family's life. A four year old needs freedom to try out new skills and interests, while at the same time needing the reassurance, safety, and support of parents. A son or daughter leaving home wants and needs freedom but may not be emotionally or financially ready to "cut the apron strings." For the family, a crisis can occur if it is required to modify its behavior significantly in order to increase a leaver's freedom. If the child leaving home has had a pivotal role in maintaining family equilibrium, it is likely the process will be more of a crisis for the family than for the leaver.

Forming a self is a lifelong process. As soon as we work with the concept of a life cycle, we become aware that human beings are always changing. Individuation always takes place in the context of a community, and it is a process never entirely finished. In that sense, leaving home is a lifelong task.

Although the process of leaving home begins near the end of adolescence, we cannot assume it is completed in young adulthood any more than we can assume that identity formation is finished in adolescence. Families that have a hard time letting go, or individuals who have a hard time leaving, may extend the process of leaving home into the middle years. Some people have said that for them the process of leaving continued until their parents died. Sometimes, even then, there is still work to do to separate emotionally from their parents. That is not surprising if we believe that the capacity and the need to grow—and even to transform ourselves—continues throughout life. Most of us are like Shanna in the story below. It takes longer to leave home than we think it should. It is, as a matter of fact, a lifelong process.

> My mother has always been the authority on good taste, interior design, style, clothes, etc. She is artistic and every house she decorates gets photographed for magazines, so her opinions on home decorating are *very* intimidating to me. I have little sense of confidence in my own taste. Recently, I bought a new home and "gave myself permission" to choose paint colors and curtain fabrics. I knew my mother wouldn't approve. She didn't. But I did it and I *like* what I did. Her critical, sometimes insidious comments don't bother me quite so much anymore. It's *my* home! I suppose at thirty seven it is about time I am free enough to differ with my mother.   (Shanna)

Development is an intellectual process as well as an affective one. In his book *The Emerging Self,* Robert Kegan weaves together the thought of Piaget with other developmental theorists to define maturation in terms of the capacity for making meaning. There is a need, he argues, for a "sophisticated understanding of the relationship between the psychological and the social, between the past and the present, and between emotion and thought."[6] Human development is more than psychosexual and psychosocial; it is the integration of intellect and affect in order to diminish reactivity and enhance intentionality.

The late Murray Bowen's theory of differentiation of self from family of origin follows a similar line. According to Bowen, the result of self-differentiation is that we are able to use our intellect to modify our response to an emotionally charged circumstance.[7] Leaving home, as the process of gaining release from the claims of one's originating family, has the effect of liberating the intellect from emotional reactivity. The process of leaving home parallels the differentiation of self in at least two ways: it sets limits on the ways in which family expectations affect the choices we make or the relationships we establish and it confirms the differentiating self by effecting new family roles.

> I was raped two years ago. I have not as yet told my family because I am afraid they will turn on the overprotective routine and sweep me back into the "safety" of home. I write to them so they do not suspect anything is wrong, but I have not given them my new telephone number. I do not want to go home for Christmas. I do not want to have any ordinary connection with my family. (Cathy)

The only way Cathy knew how to avoid being overprotected was to eliminate all meaningful contact with her family. Cathy's action is what Bowen has described as "emotional cutoff." In order to diminish family influence, the leaver feels he or she must eliminate family contact. For Cathy, separation from her family was almost all reactivity. There was little room for reason or intellect. What seemed to her like freedom is in fact even greater emotional bondage.

In order to form a self and leave home, one must be willing to experience the anxiety inherent in taking a stand against one's environment. The freedom to be different and the willingness to risk being different are essential elements in the process of leaving home. This separation, like the one at the beginning of the human life cycle, usually includes some anxiety. Adult children who are reluctant to risk this necessary confrontation in order to minimize anxiety are likely to stay stuck at home emotionally. These confrontations need not be angry outbursts. They may be very quiet and determined acts of insisting on one's point of view in a discussion with a parent or persisting in a decision that does not have parental approval or family endorsement. It is possible to leave home without ever differing openly with one's parents—but not very likely.

> The Kruse family owned their own store and lived in rooms behind the store—a self-contained business and a self-contained family as I discovered shortly after I became their pastor. They sat at the crossroads of our village and criticized everyone and everything. The entire world was wrong, the governing board of the church was wrong, the town board was wrong, the business people in town were wrong. Their daughter Marilyn was valedictorian of her high school class. She immediately took an office job in town that lasted exactly one week. With her parents' blessing, she returned to her family and took in sewing. Later I realized that Marilyn had agreed to see the world as her parents did. It would be betraying her parents if she were able to function in the world they had rejected. Whenever I encouraged Marilyn to think about doing something to utilize her obvious gifts, I was reprimanded by her parents.   (Pastor Clift)

The whole developmental plan may be hampered by an inhospitable environment that discourages risk-taking or avoids conflict. If the environment is excessively controlling, one might conclude, as Marilyn did, that confrontation for the sake of autonomy is simply too costly. We are least likely to risk being different if avoiding conflict is a family norm. We are most likely to risk being different in a context in which differentness is not regarded as dangerous and diversity is celebrated.

The development of a self is a richly varied process. Although the themes that have been identified regarding human development and leaving home have widespread application, they are not universals. There are many factors beyond one's own gift and one's family of origin that affect the process. At best, the movement toward self-definition is a pathway fraught with many pitfalls. There are also divergent views about what it means to be a family or an individual human being that modify the process of forming a self. For that reason, we need to consider how theories of human development are modified by taking gender and ethnicity seriously.

The Difference Gender Makes

Even if the beginning is the same for men and women, it is still different. Developmental theorists since Freud have assumed that the experience of the male child is normative for understanding how a self is formed. The fact that males and females experience the process of individuation differently was interpreted by Freud as women's developmental failure. Only recently have we come to understand that men and women have different developmental experiences. Those differences are not a sign of failure; they do, however, have consequences for the way in which a self is formed.

All human creatures begin life with a lengthy period of dependency. From that common, lengthy experience of dependence, we assumed that separation and autonomy were normative for human development. We now know that the differences between masculine and feminine identity are shaped by the social organization of the family that determines who the primary nurturers are at the beginning of life. The fact that a woman, even if not the mother, has been largely responsible for early child care is a significant factor in understanding how girls and boys develop into women and men.

During that emotionally intense period of dependency, our first experiences of attachment are ordinarily with a woman.

Separation from that first attachment is, however, very different for boys and girls. Girls can continue to be attached to their mothers in the process of forming gender identity, but boys must separate from their mothers and identify with their fathers in order to define themselves as masculine. Carol Gilligan points out that "since masculinity is defined through separation while femininity is defined through attachment, male gender identity is threatened by intimacy while female gender identity is threatened by separation."[8] For women, the formation of gender identity is never disconnected from intimacy. On the other hand, since male gender identity rests on manifestations of autonomy, emotional closeness is often experienced as a threat to one's sense of self.

The relationship between identity and intimacy is different for men and women. The connection between intimacy and identity in gender development parallels our conviction that human communities such as the family function best when there is a balance between being separate and being together. Both are essential. Yet there are fundamental differences between women and men in this matter. Carol Gilligan concludes that "The elusive mystery of women's development lies in its recognition of the continuing importance of attachment in the human life cycle."[9] On the other hand, the developmental story for men—that they must separate from their primary bond with the mothering one in order to establish gender identity—is a reminder that attachment is never permanent.

The ways in which men and women sort out the relationship between separateness and togetherness is significantly affected by the fact that women are ordinarily our primary caregivers in infancy.

> I was almost thirty before I actually left home, although I'd had my own apartment for several years. As the youngest of five, I had always been the "nice kid," the peacemaker, the

one who stopped arguments. One day I realized that that had meant helping the family sweep some very serious problems under the rug. "Leaving home" for me meant refusing to settle arguments anymore, and being willing to call a spade a spade. I remember now how important it seemed to me to be able to do that, and to stop doing what I'd been doing. And I remember the terror that seized me when my mother trotted out one of her laundered versions of a family incident, and looked to me for confirmation. "No," I said, "it didn't happen that way." I told the story as I remembered it, exposing a major problem the family had denied for years. I was desperately afraid that mother would reject me. I had rejected her policy of peace at any price. It was the first time anyone had to deal with me as an adult rather than as "sweet little 'Trina." (Katrina)

Katrina's story adds yet another dimension to the influence of gender on the process of leaving home. If a daughter's vision of what it is to be a woman is in conflict with her mother's, the work of identity formation may only begin after leaving home. The determination to follow her own vision may indeed mean that for a time, the "journey is home" because going home feels like giving up.

It is not easy to leave an abusive home. Clinical experience suggests that women who have been abused in their families of origin have a particularly difficult time leaving home. Their self-esteem is so damaged that they are terrified to take action. They are unknowingly trapped by a role that makes them responsible for maintaining stability in the family as a system. The sexual abuse of a daughter by a father may function to stabilize a marriage by reducing the unwanted sexual demands of a spouse. Physically abused daughters and wives often function as scapegoats of a dysfunctional family system.

I am the youngest in a family with three children and no father. So far as I can tell, I was the only person abused by my mother. Because my father wanted a boy, my mother blamed

me for the divorce. Whatever went wrong in the family was
my fault. Eventually my sisters agreed with mother and dis-
tanced themselves from me. I ran away from home when I
was sixteen in order to escape my mother's constant verbal
abuse. Ten years later and after hours of therapy, it is still difficult for me to avoid feeling that when things go wrong *wherever I am* it is somehow my fault. My sisters and my mother
don't help. They keep reminding me of things I did when I
was young. My mother has yet to see my own daughter.

(Belinda)

The mere intellectual discovery that one has played such
a part is often not enough to help a woman reject the role and
leave. After ten years, Belinda is still trapped in the patterns of
abuse that her family initiated and perpetuates. It is nearly impossible to leave home if you believe that you are responsible
for the balance and health of others in the family, and if you
leave, something terrible will happen. Guilt and shame make
one stay. Daughters and sons who have difficulty leaving an
abusive home may also be waiting for a blessing or at least
confirmation of worth from the abusing parent. Despite all the
pain her mother has caused, Belinda still longs for her approval. The experience of abuse is far less frequent for men and
more subtle. Sons are more likely to be abused by being expected to fulfill the needs of a mother for a surrogate husband
or to meet the demands of a father who wants his son to be the
athlete he was not.

Although the ways of leaving home may vary, the principal task is nonetheless basically the same for men and
women. The purpose of leaving home is not to establish gender
identity, but to effect a change in one's status or role in relationship to one's family of origin and to solidify the sense of
self that has already been formed. To accomplish this, men and
women alike need to gain enough internal confidence and emotional distance to modify their self-perception regarding their

family of origin. That process of separating is a lot easier if the family system confirms those changes in the departing daughter or son. If the shift is blurred by lack of clarity regarding gender identity or ego boundaries, leaving home becomes more emotionally charged and may be postponed indefinitely.

Ethnic Influences on Human Development and Leaving Home

Because there is a reciprocal relationship between one's inner and outer worlds in the process of human development, it is necessary to pay close attention to the cultural context of leaving home. No family exists independently of culture. The reciprocity between the intentionality of an individual and the intentionality of one's surrounding culture shapes each individual's own history. Richard Shweder maintains that psyche and culture, person and context, "live together, require each other, and dynamically, dialectically, and jointly make each other up."[10] This emphasis on reciprocity can help avoid a misplaced debate between the inner and outer world in forming a self.

The process of individuation is universal, but the way it proceeds varies from culture to culture. This diversity of perspectives not only affects the methods and manners of leaving home but the goal of the process itself. Individuation does not have the same value in a cultural context in which human nature is defined in terms of "we" more than "I." A culture in which the formula "I think, therefore I am" predominates is quite different from a culture in which the belief "because we are, I am" is dominant. In a "we are" culture, the process of leaving home takes on less urgency.

The patterns of leaving home are as culture-bound as the means and end of identity formation. In most East Asian cultures, for example, it is expected that a female will leave her family of origin to marry, but that a male never leaves his family of origin. In some branches of American Jewish culture, parents of married children expect to choose the names of their children's children. If the adult children refuse, the action is perceived as disobedience. In parts of Ireland, the oldest male child is not supposed to leave home until both parents have died. In North America, adult children frequently remain emotionally connected to their parents even though they live in a separate household some distance away. That pattern might be called "intimacy at a distance."

Whatever the cultural context, leaving home is a turning point in a family's history because it adds another member to the adult generation. The family therapist Froma Walsh has observed that when children are leaving "the focus typically follows the younger generation and their families of procreation, ignoring the three-generational, and often four-generational, interaction that continues across the life span."[11] She is correct in reminding us that even though the focus is on the individual who is leaving home, it is important not to overlook generational issues. What happened to grandmother or grandfather two or twenty years ago may have direct impact on an adult child's struggle to leave home. Consider the contrast between the two following personal reflections, the first by a white Anglo-Saxon woman, the second by a social worker whose family came from China.

> That granddaughter of mine Lindalee just announced that she was moving into an apartment of her own. Just imagine, and her with two small children! I think she's got a lot of courage. 'Course, her mother is upset. She liked it better when Lindalee moved in with them after Frank left her. But Lindalee says she wants her kids to know her as their mother, and not to get the idea that my daughter Patty is their real mother. Well, Patty doesn't like that one bit. But I just told her, "Patty, I did the same thing when your daddy died and you were two years old. Lived with my ma and pa

six months, and knew I had to find a way out." Lindalee
comes by it naturally, I told her.   (Bertha)

My grandmother was shocked, not to say horrified, that I
had decided to live with two roommates and move out of my
parents' home. I should say my grandmother's home, because my parents still live in the house my grandfather built
in the twenties. It's a very large house, and my father and
mother and two of my sisters live there, and one of my father's sisters. Grandmother is clearly in charge of it all, although my father runs the house for the most part. In the old
country, children did not move away from their parents until
they married, and sometimes not even then. It's a question of
morality, you know. My grandmother doesn't think I'm
going to turn into an immoral woman; she thinks I am an immoral woman for wanting to leave.   (Lynn)

*When there is a clash of cultures, leaving home may be
perceived as betrayal.* Leaving home usually results in greater
freedom to interact in the culture outside the home. If the values
of the host or dominant culture are in conflict with the family
and its subculture, then the process of leaving home is particularly painful. When the conflict is between the values of family
unity in the ethnic sub-culture and the individualism of the dominant culture, children like Lynn are seen as rejecting their ethnic roots by following an unfamiliar path of individuation.
Leaving home may be regarded as the greatest betrayal of all
because it is an offense to the expectations of many generations.

Sensitivity to particular ethnic subcultures should not,
however, lead us to overlook how a particular family develops
its own beliefs and values out of the interaction between its traditions and the influence of the dominant culture. Nor should
we overlook the possibility that cultural differences may be
used as a mask to hide irresponsible behavior. From the perspective of the subculture it may not be inappropriate for an
adult child to be taken care of by his parents at age twenty-

seven. But the expectation that children should stay at home may hide an adult child's slothful or addictive behavior.

> My family came from Viet Nam three years ago. There are seven children and I am the third son. We live in a three bedroom house. My parents still live the Vietnamese way. They want everybody to stay in the same house, even when the children are old enough to marry. I am twenty and a sophomore in college. I want to move into a dormitory in college so that I can concentrate on my studies. My parents oppose it. I think they want me close so I can translate for them. When I tried to explain to them about the American culture, they said "We . . . are . . . not . . . Americans. We . . . are . . . Vietnamese!" They sent me to talk to a priest but he did not help. He suggested I explain to my parents about American culture. I already tried that. Then he said I was caught between two cultures. I already knew that.   (Chau)

In situations where cultural values conflict, seeking help is itself difficult. Essentially, Chau's parents sent him to a Catholic priest (who was also Vietnamese) to be set straight. Chau hoped that the priest would see his side, and would set his parents straight. However, the priest is trapped between cultures as much as the family, and displayed little sympathy or understanding for Chau's situation. When he does begin to grasp what Chau is up against, his proposal is that the boy take an American approach and "explain to them" inside a Vietnamese framework. Chau had been trying exactly that and knew that it did not work.

The cultural factors affecting the process of leaving are buried here in ethnic loyalty ("We are Vietnamese") or in very practical tasks of learning to live in a foreign land and speak a new language. When leaving home happens in the midst of conflicting cultural values or at least different understandings of the process, ordinary transitions like leaving home are often superseded by crises of cultural transition.

There was a time in western civilization when children left home to go to work at a very young age. In the eighteenth and nineteenth centuries, they left their rural settings for work in urban settings, a pattern now repeating itself in developing countries. By the middle of the nineteenth century, children were being encouraged to stay home because early departure from the homestead often precipitated a moral crisis that the adolescent could not meet. More recently there are economic stresses that have been added to the other factors, prolonging adolescence and fostering dependency into young adulthood. Adult children who have left home return to live with their parents again. As a result, leaving home has become an increasingly complex process for parents and children alike. We turn next to a consideration of the ways of leaving home.

3

WAYS OF
LEAVING HOME

EVERYONE LEAVES home a little differently. Some sneak away. Some need to be encouraged to go. Others are quite matter of fact about it all. They simply clean out their room and are gone. These differences will be determined in part by family traditions, ethnicity, and the age and gender of the person leaving. However, even children in the same family will not depart in the same way. Each child is different and there are different dynamics of interaction between parents and children within the family at different points in its history. The way a person leaves home is the consequence of the interaction between the individual leaving and the family being left.

Because she was the first of six, Marilyn's leaving was the most traumatic for everyone. We must have known that we would never be the same close-knit family again. Marilyn simply left town and never came back to live, although she was a frequent visitor. Gerald moved out at twenty-one. Everyone agreed it was simply time for him to move on. Jeff left twice. Once when he announced suddenly that he was joining the Marines. After coming home from the service on a medical discharge, he went to Detroit for the wedding of a friend, decided he liked it, and stayed. Well in advance, Tom announced his plan to leave at age twenty and live by himself in a one-room apartment. Like everything else he has done, he did this right on schedule. When Kathy went to college, we lost our family helper. She came back home after two years and stayed four more years until she married. The second time she left was more difficult than the first. The last one to leave was the most painful of all. Meg was pregnant and not married. Her determination to live independently as a single mother was more difficult for the family than it was for Meg. Our biggest surprise as parents was that our children always did better on their own than we thought they would.   (Raymond)

This record of departures illustrates what families do not always easily recognize: children will leave the same family differently because each son or daughter is unique and because the family keeps changing as each child leaves. Leaving home is a process that involves the entire family. And the family's capacity to live with change and live through loss will in large measure determine its response to the leaving-home process. That theme will be explored in greater depth in the next chapter.

Leaving home is an experience of adventure as well as loss. People on the boundary between adolescence and adulthood face leaving home not only with excitement and anticipation, but also with apprehension and anxiety. There is a feeling of freedom and exhilaration—like beginning a new adventure. There is also unsettling fear that the job will not work out or our college roommate will not like us or that our parents will divorce after we leave. The families left behind are, more often than not, full of similar conflicting feelings; they know their children must depart but are deeply reluctant to let them go.

There are dramatic events and memorable moments of physical or emotional separation that begin and mark out the process of leaving home and family. This chapter is about those moments: how they happen, when they work best, and what is the hoped for result of effective leaving. There are three questions we need to ask about these events in relation to the formation of a self. (1) What prompts people to leave when they do? (2) What are the ways of leaving? (3) If some ways are better than others, what are the marks of effective leave-taking?

What Prompts People to Leave When They Do

In most instances, leaving home is simply the thing one does at a particular time in the developmental process. When Gerald moved out of his family in the story above, it was simply time to go. He was no longer subject to the bonds and boundaries of this particular family group. When the one leaving and those being left agree that "the time has come," the process will be sad but not conflicted. When that agreement is not present either because a child does not want to leave or parents are unwilling to let go, then the process of separation will be troubled and probably prolonged.

Some cultures mark the passage to adulthood with prescribed rituals. In traditional cultures, there are elaborate rites of passage by which boys are initiated into the new social status of being a man. For a girl in those cultures, the transition to adulthood usually occurs when she marries. In western cultures, there is a growing awareness of the need for rituals to mark these transitions. The development of those rituals will need to proceed slowly in order to take into account the new understandings of men and women.[1]

In some families, leaving home occurs in connection with some event that may not be ritualized or even noted. When a child begins college or gets an apartment or joins the military, it is generally understood that the time has come to leave home. All of these illustrations show that leaving home does not depend on a psychological readiness to separate. The time is set by some external event most often determined by each family.

For many young people in this society, the college years are a rite of passage. They involve the same three movements as the primitive rite of passage: separation from home, a time of transition in which one is likely to be wounded in a non-physical way, and the acquisition of knowledge that inaugurates new possibilities for living.[2] The separation may be more dramatic for some than for others, but going to college is always a separation of some kind because it is a death to childhood. The metaphysical wounding that occurs in the college years makes it almost impossible for a student to return to family and high school friends with any sense of belonging. The sacred knowledge that one needs to learn is that existence means something, even though jobs are uncertain and the future ambiguous.

The motivation to leave may also come from an internal impulse of the son or daughter to escape an intolerable situation. (The family's demand that a child leave home because the conflict is unbearable for the family will be considered in chapter 4.) A child's departure from home may be a matter of escape from an abusive situation or from role expectations that are controlling and limiting the freedom to grow.

> I began leaving my alcoholic family when I was about fifteen. I ran away from home several times while I was in high school. As the oldest of six children I thought that the only way out of being the family caretaker was to become the family scapegoat. By twenty, I was pregnant and then married to someone who was not Irish Catholic. I am the caretaker of my present family, and now I want to run away from my children instead of my parents.   (Darnelle)

Leaving home was not as difficult for Darnelle as being at home. Unfortunately, however, escaping from an abusive or controlling family situation does not effect the freedom that is hoped for. What Darnelle learned is that "emotional cutoff" may effect physical separation from an unhappy family situation, but the necessary work of emotional differentiation is left undone. When that occurs, we are likely to repeat the roles and expectations of the originating family. The determination to stay away from one's family often becomes such a dominant part of living that one never leaves. When the way of leaving is marked by anger, the escape from family allows very little opportunity for return. And when we cannot go home again, it is usually because we have not left yet.

Ways of Leaving Home

Although the events of leaving home usually have something to do with moving out from under the physical roof provided by parents, that kind of movement does not define leaving home. Alex lived in San Diego, California, for fifteen years while his father and mother have remained in Foxboro, Massachusetts; yet he never left home in an emotional sense. He continued to submit every significant decision to his parents for approval. Anita, on the other hand, lived within two blocks of her parents and saw them daily, and yet it is clear to both Anita and her parents that she has left home. When Anita decided to share her large apartment with a male co-tenant, she simply told her parents that she had a new housemate. The relationship was not a romantic or even a personal one, but Anita felt she owed her parents the courtesy of warning them that a person other than she would sometimes be answering the door or the telephone. Where we go is not as important as how we leave.

Every person's "leaving-home story" is unique to that person and that family. There are nevertheless certain ways of leaving that are common enough to identify. What is suggested here is not a normative typology. Yet not all kinds of leaving home are equally effective. Some kinds of leaving home do enhance the formation of a self, while others involve major compromises or resemble three steps backward for every two steps forward. Based on the leaving home stories we have heard and read, we offer the following descriptive typology.

Unnoticed leaving is characterized by the fact that while the process is taking place, its existence is either not noticed or not acknowledged. Notice is taken only after the fact. It is as though no one can say that "Bill is leaving home," but it is possible and even easy to look back and say "Bill left home." The entire family behaves as though paying attention to the process will stop it or make it worse.

Unnoticed leaving may be effective, and usually accomplishes the individual's goal of achieving physical separation "without any fuss." At the same time, it involves a kind of secrecy and mild pretense which is perhaps a family's way of avoiding some of the necessary grieving that is an important part of leaving. Thus, the person whose leaving is unnoticed will usually find that the leaving is eventually acknowledged. ("Yes, Mandy's been living in her own apartment for about two years now. We see a good deal of her, but she's pretty much her own person.") At some later time, however, particularly under stress, the family may suddenly start to behave as though the leaver were still a child in the family. The act of leaving has taken place, but the issues that go with leaving have not been dealt with. The grief—with its concomitant sadness, guilt, anger, and anxiety—is never successfully handled. Such conflict as there might be in the process is almost entirely avoided.

> My leaving home occurred when I was twenty and went away to college. My parents took their vacation that week. They drove me to my school and then drove my younger brother to his school on their way to a fishing trip in Canada. My mother stayed at the motel with my younger brothers while my father and brother took me to my dorm. My dad gave me one of those "you're on your own now" kind of looks when he left, but he didn't say anything. I said something about catching lots of fish. That first night was a little lonely but going home was never the same again. (Deborah)

What is particularly striking about Deborah's story is that

her leaving home was incidental to her parents' fishing trip both for her parents and for her. She had learned her family's lessons well. Nobody noticed that Deborah was leaving, not even Deborah. When Deborah told this story, she understood for the first time why she was so enraged at her husband when he suggested that they go deep-sea fishing on their honeymoon.

Hidden departures consist of announcing from a distance that one has left. One could call this "sneaky leaving," but there are negative connotations to the word "sneaky." The people involved behave as if a departure that could be noticed will contain so many difficulties that the only way to leave is to "go to the movies and not come back," as one leaver put it.

> When I went to college I lived at home. Finally when I was twenty-two, I moved out in the middle of the night and didn't tell anyone where I was going. Two weeks later I called my mother and told her where I was living. For six months my mother called every day begging me to come back home. More than a year later, a friend of mine called my parents' home expecting to find me there. "When did he leave?" my friend asked. To which my mother replied, "Oh, he's never really left; he's just trying out an apartment to see how it suits him."
>
> (Franklin)

It is clear that this kind of leaving avoids both the grieving process and the potential conflict in the same way unnoticed leaving does. As he quickly discovered, Franklin has reason to fear that his departure would have been prevented or aborted if he had done it in the open. The process of leaving home had to be planned and executed in secret and announced only after the fact. It has the kind of "elephant in the living room" quality seen in families where there is a major problem with some form of addiction.

Unnoticed leaving and hidden departures both involve an unwillingness to confront the grief issues that are always present in leaving. Furthermore, as long as the fear of not being able to go is not tested, those who leave in these ways have to continue to stay away. One way to understand the difference between the two is that in unannounced leaving the leaver colludes more heavily in the denial.

Leaving angry happens in a number of ways. It takes place when the departing child cites the family's inadequacies and faults as the principal reason for going. The departure is not acknowledged as coming "because it is time," but because "you people are driving me crazy" or some other angry complaint. A fight of some kind is generated and the "leaver" walks out. In some family situations, getting mad may be the only way out. And for some people the only way to leave any situation is to pick a fight and avoid the grief.

> My leaving home was very stormy. My older brother left within a month after having a fight with Dad about joining the Navy. My twin sisters had stayed at home while going to college. I wanted to go away to nursing school, but Dad said no. Dad and I had always argued about anything. This fight was different. It was very angry and mean. I threatened to go off and join the Navy like my brother and never come home again. I won. Mom understood my need to leave and promised to help me if Dad wouldn't. Two months after I left for nursing school, Dad left my mother. We never talked again. Although I had often wished my parents would split instead of fighting all the time, I felt awful when it did happen and guilty because my leaving home finally made it happen.
>
> (Ann)

Ann's story is an illustration of the complexity of leaving in anger. Since arguing and fighting had been a part of Ann's relationship with her father, it is likely that their separating would be conflicted as well. The intensity of Ann's struggle to leave home was also an indication of her emotional bond with her father. In those situations leaving angry is understandable even though it is messy. However, Ann's departure was problematic because she was her father's reason for staying in the marriage. When she left, he did too. Although Ann knew intellectually that she was not responsible for saving her parents' marriage, it took time for her to get over being angry at her father for leaving shortly after she did.

> After my father died, my brother took over the family. One day he announced to me that I was to quit college and "come home" to work in the family business. (I was paying my own way in college.) I told my brother that I would not quit college and that I had no intention of working in the family business.
>
> "You'll do as I tell you!" he blustered.
>
> "I don't have to listen to stuff like that," I answered and walked out of the house. We eventually were reconciled and I did take a year out to help with the business. But I remember how hard my heart was pounding when I told him I didn't have to listen to his abusive language.   (Kevin)

The most serious problem with leaving angry is that it places a major roadblock in the way of going home again. Successful leaving means, among other things, that the leaver is not emotionally cut off from "home." The purpose of leaving is in part to be able to return to the family in a new role, and this is possible for the angry leaver and/or the angry family only if some major reconciliation takes place. And reconciliation is seldom easy, especially in those families that harbor resentments.

There is another kind of leaving angry that is strikingly similar in its underlying dynamics to many hostile marital separations. This occurs when the "leaver" is asked to leave or is "thrown out of the house." In a sense, the difference is between angry-passive leaving and angry-active leaving. In active leaving the leaver consciously chooses to leave, and may even "trump up" a charge against the family. In passive leaving, the leaver may also wish to leave the family, but cannot reject them and must act in such a way as to force them to reject him or her. (Even this description makes the situation sound more like a matter of pure individual decision than we believe it actually is.)

Pretended leaving may look like any of the forms of leaving described above. But within a very brief period of time the leaver is once again a member of the family system in precisely the role he or she carried before.

In many cases pretended leaving is a ploy—an effort to escape one's role in the family, and to be cast in a new role, without actually paying some of the cost of leaving. Rarely if ever does this ploy work; the leaver re-enters the old role and the breach is sealed over (not, however, healed). In other cases, pretended leaving has more the flavor of practicing to leave. For some reason, the fact that it is practice cannot be acknowledged, so it is made to look like an actual departure.

> When I was a junior in high school, I promised myself I'd get out as soon as I could. I did not want to go through the endless arguments that my sister had with our parents. So I decided near the end of my senior year to join a convent. It was hard for me to admit to my brothers that I was doing this partly because they scorned religious people. I was sick for two weeks before and after arriving at the convent. When I left religious life six years later, my parents expected that I would live at home. I knew it would destroy my father if I didn't. After two years of living with them, I got my own apartment not far from where my parents live. I still talk to Mom at least once a day. I expect that will change if I get married. (Mary Catherine)

Mary Catherine discovered with the second departure how hard it was to separate emotionally from her parents. She only pretended to leave home when she joined the convent, and there is still a kind of pretense about her present living relationship. She would probably rather still be living at home except for the matter of privacy and a conflict over what is appropriate sexual behavior for people who are not married. Bringing dates home was awkward because her parents were always around, wanting to be friendly. Eventually, they would suggest that it was time for the men to leave. Mary Catherine avoided a clash over values by taking an apartment of her own. Her physical leaving home continued the pretense. She was able to keep the emotional bonds unchanged by hiding her value differences from her parents.

There has recently been an increase in the phenomenon of adult children returning to live with their parents after college or after discovering they cannot live on their own in the manner to which they had become accustomed. What may be economically motivated often has the effect of reinstating all the old rules and roles that were in operation before the son or daughter left home. When that immediate return to the old ways occurs in a family, the earlier leaving was probably just pretend. If, however, the autonomy of the son or daughter on the boomerang is honored and the new rules and roles are established for family living, then the leaving home process is in effect and will continue. When there are serious value differences between parents and their young adult children, moving back home is complex. (See chapter 5 for further discussion of this issue.)

When the son or daughter who is leaving is able to retain full emotional membership in the family with no perceptible change in role, leaving home has not happened no matter what the pretense. In ordinary discourse we speak of the child who somehow cannot leave or the parent who clings to the child and prevents leaving. It is convenient but inaccurate to speak of the matter in this way; the non-leaving is a matter of collusion between parent(s) and child that meets some aspect of everybody's needs. Sometimes the child consciously wants to leave and even dreams of going, but the departure never manages to come off.

77

That, too, is a matter of collusion, because the hidden rule the child obeys is that one must look and sound as if one wants to leave.

Occasionally a non-departure can be changed into a departure by drastic action from without so long as the external agent takes all the responsibility and the departing child is "swept off his/her feet." Chapter 6 will consider leaving home as a religious act when it is motivated by a call to serve God that frequently necessitates a separation from home.

> My separation from my family was facilitated through a religious experience. During my junior year in college, I felt called to deeper Christian discipleship. As a result, I saw myself as very different from my family. My self-worth came from outside my family. I was committed to a calling other than my family's aspirations for me: the call to be a disciple of Christ. (Todd)

Even if the reason to leave comes from "outside," the emotional work of leaving must be done. It is not enough to say that God has called or that the person "couldn't help it," having been swept away by some power or passion or purpose from outside the family. One must take responsibility for leaving. What Todd overlooked is that the emotional claims that our families usually have on us need to be dealt with directly whatever the reason for leaving home. It is especially important to sever the emotional bonds that keep us tied to our families when they share in the vision that takes us from home.

Unaccepted leaving occurs when a child leaves home and parental figures do not accept the departure but continue to treat the departed son or daughter as if she or he were still living at home under the rules of the family. What makes it genuine leaving is that the leaver consistently treats himself or herself as a leaver even though the family resists the process. Resistance to leaving home can be observed in families whose ethnic roots do not accept leaving except to marry. Other examples can be found in families adhering to religious beliefs that control individuation. It is also likely that families in which the leaver's role is essential for the maintenance of stability in the system will find myriad reasons why a son or daughter should not leave "just now."

In various forms, one can observe the conflicts in Asian-American, Hispanic-American, and other ethnic groups living on the border between the culture the family came from and the new American society, which promotes ways of leaving home that conflict with the values of the original culture. Sons and daughters in those families will leave home in ways that will not be understood or accepted by their parents.

This situation, though painful, is relatively benign when compared to what happens in religiously constricted families or abusive families. In such families, members are often frozen in a set of unchangeable roles. The role of leaver is never allowed to develop in the system. What is worse, no role is ever allowed to change, and those left vacant by a death are reassigned. Thus, a woman in her mid-thirties whose father was a minister in a very conservative religious group is still expected to be the child who makes everyone else happy. The family also now demands that she—a mother struggling alone to make ends meet and rear her eight-year-old son—must take on the mantle of her deceased mother and cook huge meals for all birthday and holiday gatherings. Although she rejects these demands in her mind, she ultimately gives in to them.

Matter-of-fact leaving consists of a simple announcement and an equally simple acceptance (at least on the surface) by the son or daughter who is leaving. The departing child announces, "I've found an apartment of my own, and I'm moving on the tenth of next month." Family members may respond with interest, with offers of help, and with some expressions of mixed pleasure and regret.

What is significant is that the entire process is out in the open and acknowledged; there is little or no conflict connected with it. Information and plans are shared by and with all the parties affected, and it is possible to allow conflicts over the leaving to surface, be acknowledged, and—sometimes—dealt with. If differences, resistances, and attempts to control the leaver are present, there is an opportunity to handle them matter-of-factly. The cluster of feelings we call grief is recognized as appropriate but often not dealt with.

Leaving Home Requires Intentionality

Murray Bowen, one of the founding fathers of family therapy, has argued that any leaving that does not involve intentionality on the part of the leaver and open communication in the midst of the process is not leaving at all. The person who has engaged in what we have called unnoticed leaving or unannounced leaving has left the family of origin less effectively than the leaver who squarely faces unaccepted leaving. The process of leaving, argued Bowen, must involve communication around the leaving, even when the communication is marked with conflict.[3]

Bowen also suggested that leaving is not something we do once and have done with; in fact, we may need to leave the family of origin several times. That process is visible in his own autobiographical essay, famous among students of family systems.[4] In clinical practice, Bowen insisted—as do his followers—that adult sons and daughters who are not sufficiently differentiated return to their families of origin in order to leave more effectively than they did the first time. This prescription may demand that a person deliberately violate the rules that had heretofore prevailed.

Obviously there are many ways to leave home. Some of the variants are determined by family rules. In some families, for example, females may be allowed to leave home in a relatively unconflicted way, while males are supposed to leave unannounced or sneak away. In other families those gender-specific expectations are reversed or linked with birth order. Being intentional about leaving presumes enough sense of self to determine a course of action. Because forming a self is an uneven process, some children who need to leave home may not have a sufficient sense of self for going unless the process is well-defined and unconflicted.

Unfortunately, we have very few rituals for leaving home. Many of the stories we have been told link that moment with a time of physical separating from our home of origin in order to move to a new city or go to college or take a job in another place. Most of the time, the leaving home moments or events that have emotional power to continue the process of differentiation are connected to ordinary incidents—like buying a new car or changing jobs or having a baby or getting married or taking a vacation or changing religious affiliation or not visiting our parents at Thanksgiving or keeping a secret or entering therapy or paying for dinner.

> The most memorable incident that occurred when I began to leave home happened before my marriage. I had been having a fight with my fiancée. I was upset. My parents could see this and they asked me about it. I used to confide in them totally, so I had to think before I said anything. My response was that it was something my fiancée and I needed to work out. Mother was sort of stunned, but my father said, "Very good." (Sam)

For the leaver, it becomes a leaving home moment when it is interpreted as one. Sam was fortunate that his father validated the moment and thereby confirmed the process. Leaving home is more effective when it is intended by the leaver and acknowledged by the family being left. But it does not always happen this way.

Because my mother always overreacts, smothering me with overprotectiveness, disapproval, or effusive flattery, I did not tell her about my serious, unexpected surgery. I was afraid she would insist on coming up to help. It is very draining for me to have her around, so I didn't tell her before the operation. I needed all my resources to survive the surgery. She has never forgiven me for not telling her at the time. It was a very bold thing for me to do, but I could not tell her why. It would hurt her too much if I said that her presence would have impeded my recovery.   (Darneather)

As we have already noted, the process of leaving home takes time. There will be many moments, which the leaver interprets as significant times of differentiating, that will go unacknowledged. Leaving home is a complex process that happens over and over again. As a former student put it, "I didn't leave when I left; I left when I stayed; and before I finally left for the last time, I was already gone."

Marks of Effective Leaving Home

Leaving home, we have said, leads to a readiness and a willingness to make one's own decisions, indeed to make one's own way in the world without undue emotional dependence on the home from which one has come. Because each of us has a unique relationship with our family, each individual journey from home is different. Still, at least within the American context, it is possible to identify some marks of the process when it is working right.

The leaver makes plans without depending on parental approval. Deciding what to do if father's birthday is on the same weekend as homecoming or planning a ski vacation over Christmas away from parents or intending to buy a car one cannot afford are leaving home decisions. Sometimes we are thrust into making plans without time to seek parental approval. But when there is time and we choose not to seek the parental blessing for a major decision, we can say we are leaving home effectively. Sometimes the difficulty leavers have in making plans is simply from a lack of practice. We learn to make good decisions and we learn from our mistakes.

The leaver may consult parents about decisions but does not feel obligated to follow their advice. Ideally, whenever we face a significant decision, we are free to consult whomever we believe will help us make a good decision. Sometimes, because sons and daughters have difficulty not doing what their parents advise, they simply do not ask. This may be temporarily necessary but it is not a desirable long-term pattern because it isolates parents and children. To be able to ask for advice without feeling obligated to follow it is a mark of effective leaving home.

The leaver does not respond to parental attempts to evoke guilt as a way of maintaining control. Stories we have heard of struggles to leave home are filled with subtle and sometimes blatant efforts to manipulate the behavior of children leaving home through a sense of obligation or guilt. It is necessary to believe that the leaver's family can get along without him or her. And even if they can't, it is not the leaver's responsibility to save them.

> When my father told me shortly before he died that the "light went out of my mother's life when I left for college," I understood more clearly why it was so difficult for me to leave home. (Herbert)

Usually parents do what they do because they intend the best for their children. Sometimes, however, their efforts to maintain control are motivated by a fear of abandonment.

The leaver does not determine his or her behavior on the basis of the expectations of future rewards or punishments from the primary family. The economic dependence that often accompanies extended adolescence makes it difficult for children to leave or parents to let go. Sons and daughters refuse gifts of

support they desperately need in order to demonstrate an independence they cannot afford. From the beginning of life, the
process of differentiation tests the family's capacity to love un-
conditionally. Being able to love without strings attached
makes it easier for children to leave and for parents to let go.

*The leaver is able to retain rich and satisfying relation-
ships with his or her original family.* We leave home so that we
can go home again. We do not mean returning to live with the
family but the capacity to reconnect in a significant emotional
way with one's family of origin. The aim of separateness for
the sake of autonomy is the possibility of community. It often
takes considerable effort to return to the home of one's parents
without succumbing to familiar and previously acceptable patterns of behavior. When we can go home again without that
happening, we know that we have been effective in leaving.

*The leaver is able to say of the place where he or she now
resides "I am home."* One can talk about "my childhood
home" or "my parents' home" or "my original home" and not
compromise the work of leaving, but it is important to reserve
the simple phrase—"my home"—for referring to the place
where one now resides. What we are saying, of course, is that
leaving home involves redefining home. This is the single most
powerful symbolic way of talking about the leaving home
process; the degree to which one is able to say this—and mean
it—is one indication of the degree to which one has successfully become an autonomous adult.

Families have a harder time accepting this than do
leavers. When someone like Kenneth's father asks the question
"Where's home for you?" it usually refers to the place where a
person lived with his or her parents in childhood and adolescence. Parents mean the same thing when they ask, "Are you
coming home?" for holidays or festive observances. If the
leaver says, "I *am* home," the parent will often say defensively,

"Oh, you know what I mean." It is not useful to turn such a comment into an argument, but it is important to recognize that what the parent really does mean is that to some important extent the parent has not accepted the child's leaving home.

The leaver is free to grieve the losses that accompany leaving home. Although leaving home is mostly a time of adventure, it is a time of loss as well. As we will note in the next chapter, the family often feels loss more keenly. Nonetheless, it is a time of loss for the leaver, too. It is easier for him or her to take the adventure if there is freedom to grieve. Prolonging adolescence, staying in the transitional phase of development, is a way of avoiding the losses that are inevitable. We have found it helpful in thinking about the losses of leaving home to organize them around some of the six types of loss we identified in *All Our Losses, All Our Griefs*.[5] Naming the experience of leaving home as loss is intended to give permission to grieve what we must give up in order to grow up.

That leaving home involves "interpersonal" loss is self-evident. One is no longer in regular contact with family members and friends from the home of one's origin. Leaving home is also a time of "intrapsychic" or "intrapersonal" loss. It is an assault on childhood ignorance, innocence, expectations of dependency, and parental omnipotence. The freedom to choose is the "burden and the gift that we receive when we leave childhood, the burden and the gift that we take with us when we come to childhood's end."[6] Because it is not possible to take all of one's childhood mementos along when one leaves, material loss is another dimension of leaving home. Familiar sights and sounds and smells are left behind. And when your bedroom becomes mother's study, the material loss is complete.

Role loss may mean nothing more than no longer thinking about oneself primarily as someone's daughter or son. It also includes setting aside the role that one had in the original family. It is sometimes difficult for leavers to let go of those roles because their own sense of self is intimately connected to being the family healer or the peacemaker or the clown or the responsible one.[7] Families are particularly reluctant to let a child give up their role if that role is felt to be essential in maintaining equilibrium in the system. While children who are leaving may think about themselves as having achieved new and more equal status in relation to parents, that change in status is something that must finally be granted. Letting children go is the beginning of that status change. It is to that family task we turn next.

4

AND LETTING GO

MY MOTHER'S death in January began one of the most tumultuous years of my life. Her dying was a mercy, but my grief wasn't easy. From early childhood I had been expected to be more than a son. It had been my role to keep her from depression. I was relieved when she died. It is not easy, I have found, to acknowledge relief in grief.

Shortly after we returned from my mother's funeral, Arvid came to live with us. He was a delightful exchange student from Denmark whose presence changed our family's dynamics more than we anticipated or acknowledged. When my wife began traveling in her new job, our daughter was often the only female in a household of males. The tensions in the house did not go unnoticed, but the changes in the family were greater than we knew.

That summer following my son's graduation from high school, we did some major remodeling of our house. In a curious way, the remodeling and the upheaval it caused were symbols of stability as well as change. We were settling down in our small city for the long haul. Meanwhile, my daughter was growing up faster than I was prepared for. It was already enough that my mother had died and my wife traveled a lot. I did not actively resist the changes my daughter was going through; I merely ignored them. Between sanding and staining doors, I also put the finishing touches on a manuscript for publication.

The carpet-layers showed up on the morning of the day we were scheduled to drive to Chicago to put our son on the train for college. We stopped at our favorite motel in Rockford on the way. We told stories around a ritual meal. But the next day, as soon as we had seen him off, we headed directly home to admire our new carpeting. It was a major blunder. We were unable to acknowledge all the changes that had occurred to the family since my mother's death. We should have stopped again at Rockford.   (Herbert)

The process of leaving home comprises two movements. The first focuses on the person leaving and on what the separating son or daughter must do to make the separation from home a constructive moment. It is a process that happens in many ways, but the end is the same: enough functional autonomy to go home again. Herbert's son was ready to leave. He had been working at differentiating for some time. The family marked the event with a modest ritual around food and story in a symbolic place, Rockford. They solidified their son's leaving home by confirming the internal changes in him that had been occurring over a period of time.

The second movement in the process of leaving home is letting go: what the family does to acknowledge the changes that have taken place, and those that must still take place in the system because one of its members is gone. In this task, Herbert's family did less well. They did not take time to reconstitute the family as a unit of three in a way that recognized the changes that were occurring. And they ignored the grief they felt. A family's unwillingness to make and to mark the necessary changes in the system usually indicates some difficulty letting go. And if the family system does not change, it is harder for sons and daughters to go home again.

Children may leave without parents letting go. And families may let go of children who would rather not leave. At best, however, the process of leaving home is transitional for both children and parents. For the leaver, it is mostly a new adventure that requires courage. For the family that is left, it is more a time of change and grief.

In this chapter we intend to explore what families do to make it harder or easier for children to leave. The motivation for impeding leaving home ranges from fear for the child's well-being outside the safety of home to the parents' dread of abandonment. If a family has a history of avoiding grief, that history will inhibit a positive response to a child's separation. It is easier to leave a family that can cope with change and live through grief. Families that can give a blessing also make it easier for children. Stable families are easier to leave.

Even When Change Is Anticipated, It Is Disruptive

Leaving home is a change that the family can see coming. Every family's life cycle has crises that can be anticipated and that occur at relatively predictable moments because natural changes are taking place. In such crises, there is grief from the losses that those changes created. There are also unexpected and unwanted changes in a family's life, and these, too, cause grief. Expressing that sadness is an essential family task.

Sometimes the changes that can be anticipated in a family's history are intensified by changes that are not expected, as happened in Herbert's family. The stability of the family may be disrupted. Because leaving home is the first major anticipated loss in a family, it is usually the first serious challenge to a family's capacity to adapt to change. How a family grieves for the losses that accompany change will enhance or impede the process of leaving home.

Leaving home may be the first loss a family can anticipate, but it will not be the last. It is inevitable that any family is both a context for change and a changing context. The family changes as its members grow up and grow older. If the family as a whole keeps changing, then it will be able to provide a nurturing environment for each of its members to grow and change from birth to death. Most families live through a variety of these changes with the normal array of bumps and bruises. Many of these changes can be anticipated, and then celebrated, ignored, or resisted. The capacity to adapt *to* change, particularly when it is unwelcome, enables a family to be a context *for* change.

Change should not be so surprising. If we believe that God is still creating, nothing that lives is finished or complete. What is true of creation in general is true of families in particular. The family is a changing organism because individuals within it change as they grow up or grow older and because the needs of the family change as a result of individual growth and altered circumstances. Nothing stays put very long, because God is always making something new. Change is part of a creation that God has declared to be good.

What a family believes about change will determine whether and how it celebrates a child's leaving as an expression of God's ongoing creative activity. Some families believe that God is the one who is always and inevitably on the side of change. Other families regard change as alien to the purposes of God. If a family's belief system depends on sameness to provide stability in human living, it is likely to regard any change as disruptive. What families believe about change will make it harder or easier for sons and daughters to leave home.

Even If Change Is Good, It Is Chaotic

Real change is chaotic even when it is necessary and desirable. It throws the family off balance, upsetting its stability. The satisfactory resolution of a major family transition such as a child's leaving home demands a fundamental shift in the structure, rules, and patterns of interaction within the system. There are at least two ways of looking at ordinary change in a family's history. One holds that families "do not change in a smooth unbroken line but in discontinuous leaps."[1] When it does occur, discontinuous change is irreversible; a family cannot return to a prior way of functioning. From this point of view, a family's ability to change requires a capacity to live with disintegration and confusion until something new emerges out of the chaos. The history of a family seen from this angle is likely to appear episodic and full of surprises.

From another perspective, change is understood as continuous and inevitable for families because it is an ongoing aspect of all creation. Everything that lives changes. Families are always changing because people do. Most of that change is so gradual that it goes unnoticed. There are, however, critical times in our lives when major transitions occur, but the outcome is relatively predictable. Families sometimes get stuck when they fail to achieve a "discontinuous leap." They can also be stymied when they are unable to complete a process of change that has been ongoing.

Change in human life and in family living is both continuous and discontinuous. Some that occur in families are so fundamental that everything changes. Those who minister to people in families are also aware of the less obvious transformations occurring all the time. These are not always easy to perceive because continuity is preserved. They are the daily shifts in attitudes, rules, and roles that families work out as members grow older. Those subtle, out-of-clear-view changes create the environment in which more major transitions such as leaving home can occur.

Not all changes in a family are constructive. Sometimes the act of leaving home itself is premature and insensitive. For the sake of an uncompromising determination to be free and independent, we may show a callous disregard for the community that nurtured us from birth. There are changes that occur in family living that are more the consequence of life-style choices than crises in the life cycle. We need to remind ourselves regularly that the unexpected changes that come because of the "slings and arrows of outrageous fortune" should not be used to undermine the conviction that change is an inevitable dimension of human life and family living. Whether the change that occurs in a family is continuous or discontinuous, a family's capacity to live through change depends on its ability to live with grief.

Change as Adventure and Change as Loss

Change in individual and family living is the occasion of adventure that can be challenging, exciting, and often scary. This understanding of change calls for boldness and a willingness to take risks. It is the promise of companionship that enables us to endure the uncertainty that comes with adventure. Lewis echoes this view in *The Chronicles of Narnia.*

> "This signifies," [said Prince Rilian] "that Aslan will be our good lord, whether he means us to live or die. And all's one, for that. Now, by my counsel, we shall all kneel and kiss his likeness, and then all shake hands with one another, as true friends that may shortly be parted. And then, let us descend into the City and take the adventure that is sent us."[2]

Change as adventure (that is sent us) contrasts with the popular notion that genuine adventures are abnormalities. Life *ought* to be smooth and predictable. Instead it is usually chaotic and full of change.

All change involves loss of some kind, even when it is also experienced as gain. Therefore, change always prompts grief. For that reason it is possible to say that a family's adaptability to change is determined by its ability to grieve. Even when the change is clearly an improvement, even when it is fully anticipated and known to be inevitable, even when it initiates an adventure we have long hoped for, still there is some sense of loss when change occurs. Where there is loss, there is grief. Adaptation to change depends in part on our ability to be sad and angry about the grief of change.

Most changes bring a mixture of adventure and loss, of pleasure and pain. The changes that occur in family life are welcome and unwelcome, comic and tragic. A leaving home moment will be anticipated with a mixture of excitement and pain. Parents who understand this sense of paradox will look forward to a daughter's wedding, knowing it will bring joy and pain as well as shifts in family boundaries that they both want and do not want. Unfortunately, some families see major changes as events to be either celebrated or hidden away. So a family may remove individuals from albums and conversations as though they had never been. Another family may faithfully mark and celebrate each major shift in its history, even at the price of considerable pain. We are most able to "take the adventure that is sent us" if we expect paradox.

There is no way to avoid change in individual or family life; what makes the difference is our response. One family may easily recover its equilibrium in response to a slight alteration, while another has difficulty coping. More significant changes, such as leaving home, forming a new family, having children, and letting them go may stretch a particular family to the point where a simple recovery of equilibrium is impossible. The same is true with the onset of chronic illness, serious injuries, divorce, death, and other trauma. It is a major task for people who work with families to assist them to notice change and then to spend time and energy reconstructing a system that will change again and again.

My husband, Shawn, and I have been married for almost twenty-four years. We have four daughters, Cybil (twenty-one), Cynthia (nineteen), Martha (seventeen), and Margaret (fifteen). Cybil and Cynthia are away at college. Martha is a senior and Margaret is a freshman in high school.

The Roman Catholic parish where we worship recently announced plans for a pictorial directory. I decided we would not have our family picture in the directory unless we could get all six of us together at one time. There was major opposition to my decision, so we set out to find a time when Cybil and Cynthia would be home from college. Every time I thought I had a time when we could all be present, someone would remember a meeting, cheerleading practice, a dental appointment, etc. Finally, on the day after Christmas at 11 A.M., we had our family portrait taken.

At some point during all the making and canceling of appointments, I realized how little all six of us are together anymore. It was *very* important for me that we have this portrait, even though the family of two parents and four "little" girls no longer exists. I bought every picture the photographer took. They symbolized a portion of life that will never be the same again. The portrait is framed. It holds us all so nest [sic] in a small space.   (Martha)

We have reported it just as Martha wrote it. The portrait kept the family framed in a "nest" against inevitable change. It was one way to keep things the same. The recovery of equilibrium is often referred to as the principle of *homeostasis,* from the Greek root meaning "to stay the same." Martha hoped for a little more sameness. *Homeostasis* exists side by side with *morphogenesis,* "to start a new form." The latter denotes the capacity of a family to move from its previous shape to an entirely new form and structure, which might not have been predictable from observing the previous family dynamics. Martha celebrated the changes in her family that meant it would never be the same again. And she grieved for them as well.

The idea of reconstitution requiring disintegration is but one of many paradoxical conditions with which we live. Family living involves continuity and discontinuity at the same time; the way to stay together successfully demands separation; people need to be loved as they are in order to be free to change. The family's task is not always to overcome paradox but to learn how to live with it and in it. Maintaining equilibrium in the family is not just preserving a negative status quo but a matter of keeping the paradox as well balanced as possible.

Grieving the losses that accompany a child's leaving home comes before the commitment to be a family in a new way. The family's ability to grieve is influenced by many factors: its history of previous loss, its beliefs about change, its willingness to be vulnerable, its understanding of the relationship between continuity and change. In order to avoid feelings of grief or the work of grieving, some families set limits on change, isolate members who are grieving, ignore changes when they occur, or make the grief a secret that must be kept buried at all costs. Sometimes such avoidance has a negative effect upon a family for generations.[3] In order to be a context that promotes growth by welcoming change, families need to learn how to grieve together.

Every Family Has a History of Loss

The response to leaving home is a continuation of the family's history of grieving other losses. Families that function well have stories to tell about significant loss and how it was handled. Each new loss in the family is linked to previous experiences in ways that enhance or prevent grieving. Families that do not function well are often stuck in grief. The stories are secret, the pain is buried, and the family recapitulates previous denial.

> It was some time after both of my children had left for college and we had moved to a new location that I discovered some striking parallels between my own leaving home for college and my son's departure. These discoveries help me

to understand why we did not stop again in Rockford. My response was in large measure a continuation of the legacy of buried grief that I had received from both my mother and my father.

In March of the year I graduated from high school, my maternal grandmother died. She had been sickly for a long time, but for an even longer time she had been a very demanding person. She terrified my mother. Nothing my mother ever did was enough. I remember my mother's guilt when her mother died. She had been my grandmother's nurse at the end. I expect my mother was relieved and then guilty about her own mother's death.

In August of that same year my parents moved from the Midwest, which had always been their home, to western New York. It was a tough adjustment for my mother. But the more difficult loss was my departure within a month for college in Minnesota. I had been her "rock of Gibraltar" and the "light of her life." She never fully recovered. The next summer, I helped admit her to a mental hospital.

Sometimes I think I carry the grief she could never fully express. At the least, I am sure that the lessons about grieving that I received as a legacy from my family profoundly affected my inability to respond appropriately to all the losses that surrounded my son's leaving home. Perhaps we did not stop again at Rockford because I wasn't fully prepared to think about what my son's leaving—or my own—meant.

(Herbert)

The parallel between this leaving home story and the one at the beginning of this chapter points to the power of a family's history of grief in shaping its response to any loss in the present; although the events are not exactly the same, the similarities are striking enough to illustrate the power of a family's history to determine how one deals with change and loss.

Not stopping at Rockford was a logical extension of this family's history of denial, which had begun long before. Significant losses on both sides of the family had been buried, disregarded, and kept secret. It was clearly understood that some things were not to be talked about and some feelings were never to be expressed. Herbert's family had a long-standing tradition of not feeling or expressing grief.

If a family's history is full of secrets, it is difficult to tell the stories that help express sadness. If sadness cannot be expressed, then leaving home is postponed, prolonged, or done in such a rigid way that it is more difficult to go home again. Families keep grief buried with set patterns of interaction designed to eliminate surprise or unplanned eruptions from the past. Human systems such as families bury grief much as individuals do, and generally with the same effect. A family's freedom to respond to loss in the present requires freedom to have emotional access to stories of the past.

> When I was nine, my mother was hospitalized for depression. I had been told whenever I made a fuss about my mother's return that I was responsible for her condition. Years later, I sought counseling in order to get out of an abusive marriage. My family, who had strongly resisted the marriage in the first place, insisted that I stay married. I was eventually divorced and began the actual leaving home process that had been derailed at the time of my marriage. As a result of therapy, I was able to reject the belief that I was responsible for my mother's depression. When I was able to begin a new marriage and enter a new business venture without consulting my father, he repeatedly approached my pastor with requests that the pastor help "get Nadine under control." In order to continue to deny his wife's depression, my father had to prevent me from growing up and leaving home.   (Nadine)

Nadine's story illustrates the power of secret shame to inhibit human growth. Often shame limits a family's access to its own history. Stories cannot be told because *the* secret story might be revealed. Aunt Mil had to get married, and to a non-Catholic, at that. Great-uncle Gottfried was arrested and hanged as a horse thief somewhere out West. There was a suicide, a divorce, and a bankruptcy that brought shame to the family. In order to keep that secret buried, even the most ordinary experience of loss like leaving home is covered over. What we identified in the previous chapter as "unnoticed leaving" is generally a continuation in the present of the family history of covering shame and burying grief.

A family's well-being depends in large measure on its ability to grieve both the expected and the unexpected changes that must and will occur throughout its history. The inability to grieve is the major impediment to leaving home. Sometimes, in order to set limits on loss and grief, families will actually seek to prevent children from leaving. If a child cannot be kept from going, a family may attempt to deny the reality of the loss by ignoring the process. And if a child is not elevated to adult status and treated accordingly, or if the system does not change to account for this new status, a family may continue to expect or even determine an adult child's continuation in the system in a way that impedes the completion of identity formation.

Our conviction that families are inclined to repeat patterns of grieving from previous generations is not new. Beginning in the middle of the Ten Commandments and repeated throughout Torah is God's self-description as the One who punishes "children for the iniquity of parents, to the third and the fourth generation" (Exod. 20:5). This is an apt description of how things happen in families over several generations. Nowhere is that more clear than in the difficulties of letting children go.

Why Families Can't Let Go

The previous chapter suggested a typology of the ways of leaving home. The intent was to emphasize the importance of noticing the change so that the leaver's departure can be celebrated as a significant moment in identity formation. When members who are left are unable to notice the change, they are likely to discourage or prevent a child from leaving. Families have difficulty letting children go for many reasons. The following five can only suggest others: when a family role is lost, when the grief is too much, when the family is so close that the boundaries are not clear, when fear of the empty nest or parental dread of abandonment by their children in the future is present, and when a blessing is absent.

When the leaver has a significant role in the family. In well-functioning families, the roles necessary to maintain the family system are equitably distributed and regularly rotated. No one person is always the peacekeeper; no one is always the organizer of family outings; no one is always the carrier and expresser of intense feeling; no one always has the last word. When roles are rotated, every family member has the chance to develop a personality with more than one dimension. As a matter of justice, no one person is saddled with the weighty responsibility of maintaining family equilibrium. Families that have experience with regularly shifting roles have an easier time imagining and making changes to adapt to a child's leaving. But if the roles are fixed, it is more difficult for the family to adapt. Families erect barriers to leaving home because they cannot imagine how they will function without Mary to lead the cheers or Tom to bear the pain or Felicity to keep everybody honest. "It won't be the same after you're gone." A simple acknowledgment in one family, becomes in another, "You must stay because we will simply not be able to manage without you here to . . . ." Sons and daughters leaving home have to contend with guilt for abandoning their particular family roles. Long after a child has struggled to leave, a family may still say, "Mark is the one who always . . . ." because that role has yet to be assigned to another member. The expectation is that Mark will return, resume his role in the family and nothing will have changed.

Leaving home is particularly difficult if the departing child has been given conflicting roles. Suppose the child who is expected to fulfill the family dream and become a famous scientist or musical performer is also the one who has been designated to keep mother happy. This child will receive a constant demand—probably nonverbal—to stay home with mother and a verbal message which says, "You are special and we have great hopes for you." Both messages carry equal weight, though one is usually kept out of direct view, but they are in sharp conflict.

> I guess I grew up waiting for the day I would be able to leave home. That is not to say my childhood was unhappy or without love. I think I just felt judged and smothered, particularly when I was around my mother. I needed to get out on my own to grow. I eventually joined the Navy in order to be as far away from my family as I could be. It is only recently that I have become aware that my parents were always proud of me. There are two pictures of me in their bedroom, one of my sister who died, and none of the other three children. Even though it has been twenty years since I left, the bedroom I had is still called Naomi's room.   (Naomi)

Naomi had always been the family star but did not know it because all of the explicit messages she received from her family were that she needed to be taken care of. If sons and daughters have been convinced that it is their responsibility to keep parents from divorcing or to effect a reconciliation if they have divorced, then they will have a hard time leaving because the family cannot let go of the role. Children may become emotional substitutes for the departed spouse or become trapped in the conflict in ways that make it difficult for parents to let them leave. Jay Haley has observed that children may become ill, delinquent, or addicted to drugs as ways of sacrificing their own life in order to keep their parents' marriage together.[4] Sometimes children are free to leave home only when their parents' divorce is final. Being the family reconciler is only one of many roles to which children are assigned in order to maintain stability in the system, but it is a particularly difficult role to give up if the parents' marriage is unstable.

When the grief gets to be too much. Even if Herbert's family had had a history of good grieving, it might still have been overcome by so much loss occurring at once. His family's reluctance to make the necessary changes that acknowledge the son's leaving home is an understandable response to an overload of grief. The experience of multiple loss or intense grief is another factor that impedes a family's adaptation to loss when a child leaves home. If the pain—or the chaos—is too much for the family to bear, the system may simply shut down. In order to avoid more pain, a family may prevent a child from going, or a son or daughter may decide not to leave home in order not to add to the family's grief.

> I had not expected my son Bob's departure for college to be so difficult. During the summer before he left, I created daily opportunities for us to be together: golf, shopping, walks. Conflict suddenly erupted when Bob asked to have an old filing cabinet in the garage that had belonged to my father. I was enraged that Bob would even ask. As September drew closer, I became uncharacteristically susceptible to tears. I had not cried since my father died. But I was the family caretaker; I had an unspoken agreement with my siblings that I would not grieve so that they could. I had also covered over the pain of a bitter divorce. It had hurt too much. I was so happy in my second marriage that it was relatively easy to ignore old pain . . . until I encountered new pain. Bob's departure precipitated my discovery that for the previous six years my life had been constructed around denying grief.
>
> (Jeffrey)

Leaving home never takes place in a vacuum. Sometimes, as in Jeffrey's family, there is a huge amount of grief in the air. It was the old, unacknowledged feelings that prevented Jeff from graciously letting go of his son Bob. When the pain of leaving and letting go taps into old grief, it may become so intense that it must be ignored. If a leaver's birth corresponds with his or her grandparent's death, it is quite likely that old grief will be rekindled in the leaver's parent. Unnoticed leaving may be the loving action of children who perceive their parents as overwhelmed with grief. In some families the presence of so much unexpressed grief becomes the excuse to keep—or at least attempt to prevent—children from leaving home.

Even when leaving home is the only visible loss a family is experiencing, it often happens when grandparents are aging and parents are becoming increasingly aware of their finitude. Middle-aged children confront their own mortality when their parents die because the buffer is gone. If the death of a grandparent was experienced as abandonment, parents in middle years may interpret the leaving of their children as abandonment as well. The parents of children leaving home are often caught between the needs of their parents and the expectations of their sons and daughters.

When the boundaries are not clear. Every family lives with boundaries, those artificial but very real dividing lines between person and person, group and group. Around the outside of a family there is a boundary, for some families thick and almost impenetrable, for others flimsy and easily crossed, for still others somewhere in between. Boundaries define psychological space.

In the family with a thick and impenetrable outer boundary, there are usually only very flimsy boundaries between individuals inside. Such families maintain their privacy and their distance from the rest of the world, but grant family members relatively little privacy: fathers choose their sons' occupations, mothers insist on a right to walk into children's bedrooms without knocking, family members are placed in almost inescapable roles such as hero, savior, fool, scapegoat, bad kid. Boundaries between people, which enable each person to develop as an individual, are blurred. Such families are often referred to as "enmeshed." Leaving such a family is often extremely difficult.

> I came from a powerfully enmeshed family. My father barely left home; as the oldest child in the family he was expected to return and solve all the emotional messes his mother had created, which in turn made his sister and brothers irked with him. My mother never left home at all. Until she was seventy years old, she lived with one or more members of her family of origin, and together they kept alive the family system she learned in that family. That is how my mother understood family loyalty. Her family system rules had complete dominance in our family. (That may have been a relief to my father, since the rules in his family were even more poisonous to healthy development.) My mother had immense difficulty in letting me go, difficulty matched by my own difficulties in leaving. I did better when it came time for my own children to leave home, but my success was only partial. (Kenneth)

The leaver may encounter subtle or not-so-subtle statements that the child is not ready to leave. (The family will not say that they are not ready to have the child go.) Kenneth's mother couched her demands not to leave home in vague but powerful appeals to loyalty. On the other hand, she expected Kenneth to become individuated enough to be successful in the larger society. Such double-binding blocks effective leaving home.

Double-binding maneuvers are a clear reminder that change in the individual and change in the system take place simultaneously and are related to each other. Changes in the way children see themselves and in the way their families view them are mutually dependent. Both parents and children are individuating. Both are leaving behind a previous way of living and relating. Leaving home is intimately related to letting go. Helm Stierlin calls this "co-individuation," mutuality between parents and children, both moving toward higher levels of individuation.[5] The family system as a whole must change in order that one of its members may achieve greater differentiation and deeper relatedness.

Empty nest fear and the dread of abandonment. The fear of the "empty nest" prompts some parents to create obstacles to leaving home, especially when it is the last child's turn. This dynamic is particularly powerful for any woman whose primary identity has been housewife and mother. The fear of meaninglessness or emptiness in one's life after a significant role loss can prompt people to maintain old dependencies in order to be needed. Parents then treat sons and daughters as if they owed it to parents to provide them with a reason for being. Ellen Goodman describes how this is a major transition even for mothers who work outside the home:

> A long time ago, I thought that mothers who also had work that engaged their time and energy might avoid the cliché of an empty-nest syndrome. A child's departure once meant a mother's forced retirement from her only job. Many of us assumed that work would help protect us from that void. Now I doubt it.
>
> Those of us who have worked two shifts, lived two roles, have no less investment in our identity as parents, no less connection to our children. No less love. And no less sense of loss.
>
> Tomorrow, for the first time in 18 years, the part of my brain that is always calculating time—school time, work time, dinner time—can let go of its stop watch. The part of me that is as attuned to a child's schedule and needs as it is to a baby's

cry in the night will be no longer operative. I don't know how easy it will be to unplug. What do you do with all the antennae of motherhood when they become obsolete?[6]

This can be a frightening time for a couple who have paid little attention to their relationship during the time of parenting. Not so long ago, one parent would in all likelihood be dead when the last child was ready to leave home. Today, couples spend most of their married years without responsibility for parenting. Therefore, it is important for them to continue to work on being married even while primarily involved in parenting. In the fourth volume in this series entitled *Promising Again,* we will explore in greater detail what husbands and wives can do to "get married again" when the last child leaves home.

Fear that children will abandon their parents causes some couples to hold on to children long past the appropriate time for letting go. The children, parents fear, will leave and never come back. "You will become famous and forget all about us." Sometimes that happens when grown children ignore their parents because they are busy or because their parents are too needy. Sometimes home is such a destructive place and parents are so controlling the only way children believe they can survive without further abuse or suffocation is to leave and never come back. We have said that the purpose of leaving home is so that we can go home again, which is to return to the home of our origin. Most children do that. But for some people, their family is a dangerous or unfulfilling place to be. When they leave, they are not likely to return until it is safe.

The absence of a parental blessing for the journey. This is perhaps the most subtle impediment to leaving home. Because there is an intimate connection between the authority to bless and the power to control, sons and daughters who are waiting for a blessing continue to give their parents inordinate power and influence so that the blessing will be efficacious when it comes. Parents, even if unintentionally, withhold their blessing as a way of keeping control. The absence of blessing is a major obstacle to leaving home, and the giving of a blessing is the grace of letting go with love. If a child does not receive a blessing, the movement into mature adulthood is often contaminated by conditional acceptance or the preoccupation with approval by parents or even by surrogate parents.

> When I was growing up, I knocked myself out overachieving in any and every life event, hoping finally to please my father and earn his blessing. I lived for his approval. I longed to hear him speak anything that sounded remotely like a blessing. . . .
>
> As an adolescent and young adult, I blamed him for not giving me what I could not give myself, his blessing. He himself had never been blessed by his father, but I blamed him for not giving me something he did not have to give. When it came to blessings, our family existed in an economy of scarcity. . . . I channeled my rage into oedipal competition with my dad, and won often enough that we are more enemies than friends during that period. . . .
>
> My call to ministry was in part my calling out to God, the Father, asking "Him" to bless me. Through God's church I have been blessed. . . . enough to let my dad off the hook. We have arrived at a peace based on mutual acceptance and forgiveness for "crimes" both committed and never committed.[7]

All of life is sustained by the blessing of God. It is the power that makes the human soul grow and prosper and do its work in the world. Blessing, as Claus Westermann has observed, is the "vital power without which no living being can exist."[8] God's blessing also makes community possible. Nobody wants to live a life that is unblessed, without the special words and gestures that bind that life to a precious past and promised future. Those who do not have a blessing are empty-handed; they have no past to which to return and no future toward which to move. Jacob's blessing (Gen. 27–28) was achieved by deceit. It is not surprising that it continued to trouble him until he wrestled with the angel at the ford of the Jabbok; only then could he go home.

Blessing: Letting Children Go with Grace

A blessing, divine or human, begins as an acknowledgment, a recognition that the person being blessed has a distinctive identity. A blessing may not necessarily say, I approve, but it always says, I recognize. It acknowledges that the person leaving home is a separate and distinct individual, worthy of respect.

A blessing acknowledges that there is a particular order in the family and a person with authority to bless. Every family has its priest. The absence of a blessing from the family for the one leaving is not just an effort to sabotage separation but also a reflection of a much wider decline of a healthy concept of authority within human communities such as congregations and families. When a member of the family leaves home with a blessing, the authority to become a priest in one's own household is conveyed by this act.

A blessing conveys a wish for the leaver's success. The original Greek root used for blessing in the New Testament implies happiness. A thirty-year-old son said it this way, "I only wish my parents were happy because I am happy." In a blessing there can be no secret hope that the leaver's world will collapse, that the leaver will learn some kind of painful lesson and will have to return home. The blessing contains the expectation or hope that the leaver will be able to "go it alone" successfully. One mother remembers it this way:

> As we grazed through our last lunch together, my daughter said, "This is exactly what I want to be doing now." Hours later, with tears in my eyes, I hugged this tall young woman in front of her new dormitory and said, "Go fly."   (Sylvia)

"Go fly." It is a wonderful blessing precisely because it conveys an expectation of success and a hope for happiness.

A blessing is a ritual of continuity. It reaffirms ties between parents and children that will naturally remain. It binds us to a precious past that invites our return. It is confirmed not because we have earned it but because we belong to a particular people with a particular history. A blessing ritualizes a change in membership in a family, not severance from it. We love our children when we let them go. Because we love them, we let them go. That is what we mean when we say that blessing is "letting go with grace."

A blessing is a prayer for protection. Even when parents celebrate the changes occurring in their children, and even when the children welcome change as an adventure, leaving is still a time of uncertainty, of opportunities, and of dangers. When daughters or sons have received blessings as they leave, they are free to move into an uncertain future without hidden expectations that tie them to their parents or their past. Those who receive a blessing are more likely to experience life satisfaction as adults. The blessing is a ritual recognition for both parents and children of God's promise to accompany us into an uncertain future. It is remembrance of the promise of God's companionship that enables us to "take the adventure that is sent us."

Leaving home is an emotionally charged event in family life, one for which there is no ritual to help us through a boundary-crossing time. There was a time when puberty rites were the ritual of entry into adulthood. The extension of adolescence has eroded the significance of confirmation or bar mitzvah as rituals of transition into adulthood. Congregations are in a position to foster the development of new rituals that will help individuals and families transform the process of leaving home into one of the significant times of our lives.

Sometimes a blessing will occur spontaneously as it did for Sylvia when she told her daughter to "Go fly." Sometimes it will come at the end of a farewell family meal. Sometimes it will be a part of a carefully planned walk in the woods. It may include the rehearsal of leaving home stories from previous generations. Maybe there will be awkward efforts to offer an enduring maxim or to say something that children will remember. If there is a blessing, the essential components include:

—I (we), having authority in this family,
—recognizing that a change is imminent,
—wishing for your happiness without reservation,
—placing you under God's constant protection,
—celebrating your gifts,
—confirming your separateness,
—and reaffirming our enduring connectedness.

Our appreciation of the need for a blessing when we are leaving is enhanced by the awareness of the various small blessings we experience in ordinary life. We say "God be with you" —the original meaning of "Good-bye"—when we think a moment calls for a blessing, usually because of events or forces in tension with each other: separation and attachment, change and continuity, autonomy and dependence. Whether a separation is mandated by bedtime, by the kairos-time of maturity, or by the moment of death, a blessing is appropriate, and every Christian is ordained to this priesthood.

It Will Never Be the Same

Most families survive the leaving-home crisis. When the leaving is publicly marked and the family grieves its loss, the destabilizing effect is minimized and the family reorders itself. Even if members ignore the impact of a child's departure, even if they fail to "stop again at Rockford," families eventually recognize that "it is not like it used to be." The phone does not ring as often, or the paycheck (if the child was college-bound) does not last as long, but the milk and the gasoline go farther. Siblings still at home may get more attention and more space. If the leaving is unnoticed, the time for adapting to the change just takes longer.

Children will usually leave home despite parental protests or subtle manipulations. Parents who are reluctant to let go may only succeed in contaminating a son or daughter's first weeks or months away with sadness or worry. Children who have left home may discover guilt hidden away in the luggage their parents gave them. If the departure was acrimonious, nothing may change except that parents are relieved. The family—they may insist—will be more peaceful now that the troublesome one has left. It has been said that adolescence was invented to make it easier for parents to let children go.

Children leave home because they must, but it will never be the same. Even if they never live far away from parents geographically, it is necessary that parents give up the power to set the direction of an individual's life. Leaving home, we have suggested, is defined by the readiness and willingness to make one's own decisions, to make one's way in the world, without undue emotional dependence on other members of one's original family. That internal and interactional development is solidified if there is a corresponding change in the child's status in the family.

Families must change because children leave, and families must change so that children can leave. For those leaving, it is a time of adventure and the possibility of surprise. Parents may find it easier to let go if they believe that God accompanies those who are leaving. That is the promise that comes with change. The One who is on the side of change is also by our side wherever we are, in our families or by ourselves.

5

HELPING CHILDREN
LEAVE HOME,
HELPING FAMILIES
LET GO

WHEN THE PROCESS of leaving home works well, it
will probably look something like this. The son or
daughter's departure is noticed and appropriately ritualized.
Everybody has freedom to grieve the losses that are occurring.
Blessings are given and received. Children are not looking over
their shoulders as they leave. In the end, there is enough change
in status so that parents and children call one another friends,
sons and daughters are free to establish permanent relationships
of intimacy, and mothers and fathers renew their promises to
one another.

Even when leaving home goes right, however, the process
will take longer for one than for another. For some people there
may be one dramatic crisis or ritualized departure that continues to be actualized over and over. Others are able to mark a
number of ordinary events that have the cumulative effect of
solidifying their emerging sense of self. Still others may become aware that they have finally achieved an emotional separation after a long internal struggle to claim their autonomy.

Leaving home does not always run smoothly. As we have
noted already, both parents and children can get stuck in the
process at a number of points and for a variety of reasons. The

opposition to children separating is so predictable that the process of leaving home is not likely to occur without some opposition from family forces promoting togetherness. In one sense, that opposition is understandable because the emotional bonds established between parents and children during the early years of dependency are not easily changed. When we have been part of a home, it is hard to leave. Leaving home as part of forming a self will always be a struggle.

There is another kind of togetherness that generally turns the individuation process into an emotional tug-of-war. It resembles intimacy, but in reality is a kind of emotional bondage that limits leaving home. Sometimes this excessive closeness is the result of a collusion between parents and children. Sometimes it is parents who cannot let go. Sometimes it is the adult children who cannot leave. In any event the result is an emotional fusion that is not easily severed.

> Not long before I turned forty I had a phone conversation with my mother that changed my interactions with both parents. They were trying to decide whether to sell their house and move into a retirement complex. I agreed with the move. My mother had called me to elicit my endorsement of her reluctance to move into an apartment. I had just read an essay by Murray Bowen, "Toward the Differentiation of Self in One's Family of Origin,"[1] and I was determined not to be caught in a triangle with my parents once again. So I told my mother that I would not talk with her about the proposed move unless my father was on another telephone. In retrospect, it seems like a small act, but my mother was hurt and I was shaking when the phone call was over.   (Herbert)

Herbert had physically left home two decades before, but it took this conversation, after a long internal struggle, to claim enough autonomy to change how he responded to his parents. It was for him a critical moment in a protracted leaving-home process that had been complicated by an emotional fusion with his mother in particular. The moments that effect emotional separation are often unexpected and seemingly insignificant. A short phone call for Herbert turned into a moment of emotional separation that altered the course of his leaving home.

Ordinary Moments Reveal Incomplete Leaving Home

This chapter is about ways of helping further leaving home when the process gets stuck. Parents who want help for a departing son or daughter usually do not see any need to change themselves. Leavers who seek counsel far away from their parental home believe that their parents are unwilling or unable to let them go. Occasionally, parents and children will all agree they need some assistance getting through this major transition in the family's life. The family's willingness to seek pastoral counsel as a whole is most likely when parents want their children to leave before their children are willing to go.

People frequently discover unresolved issues about leaving home while seeking help on other matters. When a parent dies, for example, a son or daughter in middle years may flounder in a grief laced with personal bewilderment and identity confusion because that parent's death occasions belated autonomy. Marital conflict may be precipitated by the fact that one spouse is still emotionally entangled with his or her parents. Tension in families about child-raising practices is sometimes only a thinly veiled struggle to retain loyalty to one's family of origin.

Loving means letting go. That conviction is an extension of the promise of liberation that sustains every personal and religious journey. "For the person who has learned to let go and let be," Meister Eckhart, the fourteenth century theologian, once said, "Nothing can ever get in the way again." Letting go is something parents have to learn. We do not need to learn how to hold on; it seems to come naturally. However, we do need to practice loving and letting each other go. The greatest gift that parents can give their children is to love them tenderly and fiercely and to let them go respectfully and graciously.

There are four ways in which stuckness in the leaving home process is likely to manifest itself in ordinary pastoral ministry: (1) when parents seek help getting their under-functioning child to leave; (2) when adult children seek pastoral assistance with the process of leaving home; (3) when incomplete differentiation is hidden in marital conflict; and (4) when the impact of the death of a parent becomes the occasion for autonomy for middle-aged sons and daughters. The next volume in this series will focus on the relationship between leaving home and becoming married.

When Adult Children Are Reluctant to Leave

It has become commonplace for adult children who have left home to discover that they cannot make it on their own. We call them the "boomerang generation." Frequently the reasons are financial. They cannot live alone on the income they earn. Sometimes the economic constraints are aggravated by life-style expectations. They cannot manage to live on their income in the manner to which they had become accustomed. When the reason why sons and daughters never leave or come home again to live is primarily financial, it is easier for parents and children to work out the living arrangements in ways that do not impede the emotional process of leaving home—even while living at home. Physical proximity makes emotional separation more difficult but not impossible. It simply takes more intentionality.

Adult children who have never left or return home for other than financial reasons present a difficult dilemma for parents who are willing to let them go. Intentionality is not enough. Even when parents are eager for adult children to leave, their interaction within the family system is one of the factors that makes clear separation hard to achieve. When they look for help, however, parents are usually looking for support rather than their own self-examination.

> Sandra and I called Pastor Carlson for help with our son Mark. He just could not keep a job. The last time he lost a job, I had to fire him. His own father! Mark's been in pastoral counseling for three years, but he still gets terrifying anxiety attacks. Granted, the attacks have become less frequent, but his work performance hasn't improved. So we called Pastor Carlson. She doesn't really know Mark, but since she's been working on wedding plans with Carolyn, Mark's younger sister, we thought maybe she could help.

> In preparation for the meeting with Pastor Carlson, I had our company attorney draw up a financial agreement with Mark. It is so baffling to us that Carolyn is a successful bank manager, but Mark can't keep a job for more than six months. During the meeting, Mark accused us of being stingy. Sandra coddled him, as usual, but I pointed out that it was high time Mark buckled down and made something of his life. He is, after all, twenty-eight years old. We were sorry we hadn't done this sooner. I explained to Mark that all he needed was for us to untie his hands and let him do his own thing. Both Sandra and I are confident that he will succeed if he sets his mind to it.

> We wanted Pastor Carlson to witness the agreement with Mark that had been drawn up by my company attorney. Without getting into the legal details of the contract, it simply stated that we would not provide Mark with money for any purpose, make him any loans, pay any bills, or provide him with employment. He will get severance pay from the company, health insurance for six months, and we'll pay all his expenses to attend a vocational assessment program. I told Mark that we were confident he would find his objective and succeed once we untied his hands.

> Mark signed it and left the pastor's office immediately. We thanked the pastor for her support and promised to let her know when Mark got a new job.   (Stan Peterson)

As evidenced by Stan's story, parents may want help effecting the departure of a son or daughter, but do not see the need for personal change. It is not always easy for them to acknowledge that the interaction between over-functioning parents and under-functioning children can impede the formation of a self and subsequent emotional separation from one's original family. Stan thought the tone of their agreement with Mark was optimistic and positive. From his perspective as a father, he and Sandra just wanted their son to be successful. They knew Mark was bright and mature enough to find a niche in life. He could find security, happiness, and personal satisfaction if he only tried. Mark, on the other hand, must have viewed those expectations as punitive demands. His willingness to sign the agreement signaled more flight than freedom. His best would never be good enough for his father. The signed agreement between Mark and his parents was not a blessing. A response from Stan and Sandra that modified their expectations of Mark would have been more affirming.

Mark was under-functioning; his parents and sister were supporting that behavior and Pastor Carlson was called in as parental support. She had heard their frustration about Mark's irresponsible behavior on several occasions. Moreover, the pastor knew how difficult it had been for Sandra to let go of her children. There had been some major tensions in planning Carolyn's wedding. Sandra had managed the family and cared for the children while Stan spent most of his days keeping the family business going and playing golf.

Pastor Carlson was co-opted into witnessing the legal agreement. One of the predicaments of pastoral ministers is that they often have more access to families at pivotal moments of transition than they know what to do with. In those situations, people are more likely to expect support than challenge from their pastors. The Petersons were not looking for confrontation. As a result, therapy may be necessary to help families like the Petersons confront a systemic flaw without experiencing immobilizing shame. Later in this chapter we will suggest some principles that might inform a family ministry that does not presume therapeutic expertise.

When Adult Children Seek Help Leaving Home

There are many reasons why young adult children seek help in relation to the lingering influence of their parents. Young adults living and working away from their places of origin continue to struggle over leaving home issues when their parents insist that they "come home" for vacations or holidays. Sometimes immobilizing low self-esteem at work or at play is a signal that individuation is incomplete. Patterns of behavior that have been labeled as codependent are a continuation of roles from family of origin. In such instances, there is clearly an absence of the one characteristic of effective leaving home: the change in status in relation to one's original home. That change in family status is granted by one's family; it cannot simply be had on demand. And sometimes it never happens. Consider this story of a loyal son's determination to leave home against tenacious opposition from his parents.

> I had been a dutiful son and lived at home while attending a university thirty minutes away. After graduating from college, I began working as a staff accountant for a large CPA firm. I soon felt the pressure of living at home very keenly. I attempted to discuss the possibility of leaving with my parents in indirect ways. Every time the subject was presented, my parents communicated to me very clearly that they would be scorned as unfit parents by their families if any child left before getting married. So I stayed and consoled myself with all the money I was saving.
>
> After a year and a half, the pressure got too much. I began to look for an apartment in secret. With the help of a priest from the parish, I found something I could afford that was far

enough from my parents' home and close enough to my place of work. My parents were shocked and angry when I announced I was moving into an apartment. The first thing my father said was that "renting is below your dignity as a Fogerty." If I left, they assured me I would not be welcome back because of the shame I had caused them by leaving. They felt betrayed when they asked the priest of their parish for help keeping me at home and he informed them he had helped me find the apartment. They did not return to that parish.

The day I left, my parents watched as a friend and I moved my clothes and a few objects from their house. After one year in that apartment, I *did* move into a house, where I lived for four years. Both were about thirty-five minutes from my parents' home, but they visited me only three times in five years, despite numerous invitations. And although nothing was ever said by my parents to the pastor who had helped me get an apartment, they switched to another parish not long after I left home.   (Daniel)

According to the principles by which the Fogertys had ordered their family's life, the only valid reason for leaving home was to get married or join the military. Anything else was a mark of shame. The priest did not know all the family rules he was violating when he responded to Daniel's request for assistance. Had the pastor known, he may have prevented some hostility by avoiding the secrecy. He might have recognized how difficult it is for the parents when children leave home. Empathy, however, would probably not change the "Fogerty policy." Inevitably, the pastor's choice to stand on the side of Daniel's freedom to leave home was risky. In this instance, it meant that the parents felt they had to leave the parish.

When Unfinished Leaving Home Leads to Marital Conflict

Buried grief is often a source of conflict in marriage. That grief may be well-hidden behind ordinary things like how money is spent or not spent, what is done on holidays or vacations, the size of the long distance telephone bill, how children are to be raised, who comes to dinner, or who carries out the garbage. Frequently these tensions are the residue of unresolved emotional separation from one's home of origin. In one sense, the issue is loyalty. From another angle, however, both a family's unwillingness to let go or a child's reluctance to leave may stem from an inability to grieve the losses connected with leaving home.

> Ellie and I were married two years after we graduated from high school. I worked for my father in his auto dealership; Ellie worked in a dentist's office, and we lived in an apartment near where my parents lived. We had a good life: good friends, good family, good jobs. I was particularly glad that Ellie and my mother Barbara got along very well. They shopped together and my mother was trying to teach Ellie how to golf. However, there was one thing in this happy picture that Ellie did not like. My mother had a key to our apartment and could and would enter without knocking or without ringing the doorbell. Whenever Ellie complained, I would shrug it off by saying there is nothing I can do: "She's my mother."

> After three years of being annoyed, and not long after we had moved into a new town house, Ellie got mad and changed the locks. When my mother discovered she had been locked out of my house, she called me at work and insisted that I make Ellie apologize. In order to prevent a big fuss, I told my mother I would make her a new key. When Ellie found out what I had promised, she hit the ceiling. If I made a key for my mother, she said, she would leave. For her it was that simple. I thought Ellie was making too much of a small thing, but my bowling buddies agreed with Ellie. It wasn't until I talked to my pastor that I remembered how annoyed I used to be when my mother would clean out my closets. I had grown up believing that I was not entitled to private space, at least where mother is concerned. With a little encouragement from my friends, I told my mother she

was always welcome in my house, but she would not have a
key. The next week my father gave me a raise at work.

(Robert)

Ellie's ultimatum forced Robert to make a necessary
choice, which he had been avoiding. It is almost as if Robert had
been waiting for someone to give him permission to retrieve
what was his own. This would not be the last such choice that
Robert would have to make but the rest will be different because
he did not give his mother a key. Straightforward support and encouragement on behalf of leaving home may be all that is needed
in many instances to effect the resolution of marital conflict.

The emotional ties to the home of origin and the claims
of parents may continue in a marriage because incomplete individuation is hidden behind religious convictions, an accommo-
dating spouse, or easy compatibility between married children
and their parents. In the following situation, Arline assumed
that a bold letter written early in the marriage had effected all
the separation that she needed.

> I had not realized what a dominant force my mother was in
> our family and in my life until I married. When my mother
> would point out "grievous" faults in my husband, I would
> side with her sometimes because I agreed with her, but often
> because it had always been difficult for me to oppose her
> wishes. I had learned over the years how to keep the peace at
> any price. My husband became more and more alienated
> from my parents. It usually took several weeks for us to re-
> connect after we had been with them.
>
> As my husband and I grew in our faith, I realized that my
> mother's critical spirit was hurting both my husband and our
> marriage. With the help of my pastor, I wrote my mother a
> letter to this effect one Christmas season. I was terrified that
> my letter would cause a separation between us, but it didn't.
> My mother was less critical of my husband after that, but
> nothing was ever said about the letter. As I look back on the
> experience, I thought that I had finally left home.

About twelve years after the "Christmas letter," my mother and father came to help us move. My father took charge of our family devotional life and my husband felt displaced. My mother took over the packing and I felt invaded. While they were at it, my parents began to criticize the diet that my husband and I had been following to correct a medical problem. It seemed to me that they were trying to drive a wedge between us.

Finally I could contain my anger no longer. I stood up on the table and told my parents it was not their responsibility to tell us how to live. They were hurt and threatened to leave. We prayed together, but the air was still heavy. I was sure my parents felt I was dishonoring them. From my perspective, I had done what I needed to do to protect myself and my family from invasion. My mother did not speak to me again while we packed up the house. When they were leaving, my dad looked at me, grinned and said: "I didn't think you had it in you." That was the best blessing I had ever received from my father. As soon as my parents were gone, my husband and I had the best sex of our marriage.

(Arline)

Leaving home does not get any easier later in life. Even when the inability to separate emotionally from parents is a problem for a marriage, it is not often self-evident to sons and daughters what must be done. One might guess that Arline's husband knew what needed to change. He is to be commended, however, for not doing the work she alone needed to do with her mother. Sons and daughters who have not left home often use a spouse to say what dare not otherwise be said or to break the family rules. Doing the leaving-home work of a spouse is not useful, but it does help the leaver to have a spousal ally when the process of leaving home is particularly complex.

For many married couples, however, the process is neither as simple or as straightforward as it had been for Robert or Arline. In the previous chapters we have identified some of the roadblocks to leaving home. Families who cannot grieve will set limits on the amount of loss they will allow in an effort to lessen their grief. An adult son or daughter's need for parental approval may compel compliance and accommodation. Even when adult children know they must take specific steps to disengage from their family of origin in order to save a marriage, they may not have the ego strength necessary to act.

For many years, the family therapist James Framo has used parents as consultants in helping individuals and couples gain greater clarity about and freedom from the ongoing influence of their families of origin.[2] The intent of the gathering is not to fix blame or make accusations but rather to help family members deal with one another in more effective ways. This method is not recommended if the family system is highly conflicted and volatile. If, however, there is good will among members, a family-of-origin gathering may clarify misconceptions, diminish fear and distance between parents and children, or begin a process of reconciliation. Even when all seems to go well, meeting with parents and siblings does not work magic. It can, however, enhance ongoing family-of-origin therapy by reducing unnecessary impediments to healing.

This method is often of particular value to pastoral ministers who already have access to entire families as a part of everyday parish ministry. It serves to make explicit what is already implicit in pastoral relationships. Families come together around major ritual events or because of a death or some other crisis. Helping family members talk with one another on those ritual occasions may introduce new alternatives for family living. Ministers also have the opportunity to create structured contexts so that families can communicate with one another across generations in order to help each other. Such structured meetings have the potential to effect significant change within persons, couples, and between parents and children. It is also possible that these changes can carry over to succeeding generations.

When the Death of a Parent Causes Greater Autonomy

When a parent dies, a son or daughter in middle years may flounder in a grief intertwined with personal bewilderment and identity confusion because it is the occasion for belated autonomy. After her own mother's funeral, a woman of fifty was heard to say, "Now I feel on my own." If the process of leaving home has not been resolved until the death of one or both parents, the grief of middle-aged sons and daughters is complicated by relief and guilt. While the grieving son or daughter may discover greater freedom for self-assertion and autonomy, the death of a parent often immobilizes adult sons and daughters who do not trust their capacity for independent choice or action.

> I was thirty-six when my father died. Usually when I planned to do something like change jobs, buy something major, maybe invest in something, my first action was to go to my father. I trusted his opinion a lot. Since he died last year, I am finding it more and more difficult to make decisions. We've been looking at new cars for three months. I even signed the papers on one and the next morning I called and cancelled. I just wasn't sure if it was what we wanted. And I think this is one place where I would have called my father and he would have told me what to do. I think that's all I would have needed. My father's advice is something I really do miss, I really need. . . . He made so many wise decisions for me. . . . I don't feel that I had that much dependence on him, I just trusted him.   (Richard)

Richard's self-perception about his personal autonomy may not be altogether accurate. Indeed, there is a fine line between dependence and confidence in a designated authority. Because children often make parental values their own, the influence of parents does not necessarily end with death. Richard's inability to make decisions after his father died indicates that he does not trust his own judgment as much as he had trusted his father's wisdom. Making an independent judgment was even more difficult for Richard after his father's death.

For Richard, his father's word was almost always a positive thing. Sometimes, however, a parent's critical and demanding voice is not silenced, even in death. As a result, excessive parental domination lasts beyond the grave in ways that continue to inhibit the development of autonomy. Middle-age sons and daughters may fear the judgment of a dead parent as much as if the parent were still alive. A woman in her forties still hears her mother criticizing her from the grave. While she regularly puts flowers at her mother's grave, she still hears the same accusation: "Well, Dorothy, you finally got around to it." The process of leaving home is often seriously stuck when parental dominance extends beyond death.

Ordinarily, doing grief work with daughters and sons who have lost a parent is not fundamentally different from helping anyone grieve the loss of something or someone they have loved. Even if the death occurs at the end of a rich and full life, there is inevitable sadness when a parent dies. If, however, that death occurs before the formation of a self has been solidified by means of the process of leaving home, the grieving is more complex. If becoming one's own person or feeling free to exercise appropriate freedom of thought or action finally occurs because a parent dies, we need to be alert to the possibility that the grief for a parent's death is likely to include a disproportionate amount of guilt.

Ways of Caring

This brief survey of situations complicated by incomplete differentiation suggests several distinct modes of pastoral care. When a young adult living some distance from his or her parents seeks help with the leaving home process, the pastoral strategy most closely resembles coaching. Those who work with people in families frequently use this metaphor to describe what they do to promote differentiation.[3] It is an apt image.

Counseling as coaching keeps the focus on the leaver as the primary actor. When they are afraid of displeasing their parents or when their parents are larger than life, daughters and sons may perceive developing a plan for leaving home as something like strategizing to slay a dragon. The counseling work that needs to be done with the one who is leaving will include identifying an achievable goal, developing strategies for achieving that goal, rehearsing a plan, encouraging action, and celebrating victories small and large.

When the forces opposing separation persist in powerful ways, as in the case of the Fogertys, some pastoral assistance may be needed in removing major obstacles. However, because leaving home is something that one must do for oneself, too much advocacy with a family on behalf of the one leaving will undermine the work the leaver must do. It is axiomatic to insist that our pastoral strategies be on the side of liberation. Pastoral support for children leaving home is an extension of the conviction that responsible freedom is one goal of the process of individuation.

Pastoral interventions around leaving-home issues are respectful of the autonomy and dignity of each person. They are also supportive of the necessity for maintaining the family as the fundamental human community. It is a delicate task for helpers as well as families to balance individual needs and family needs. Because the deeper truths of life and faith are almost always paradoxical, those who engage in pastoral care must be able to see the other side. This is particularly important when the action being supported—the action of leaving home that must be taken—is perceived to be against the other side, namely, the parents who are reluctant to let their children go.

Between Empathy and Advocacy: A Delicate Balance

In both Stan and Daniel's stories, the pastoral response needed to be a delicate balance between empathy for the parents' struggle to let go and advocacy for the sons' need to leave. Neither of the pastoral responses in these situations maintained a balanced perspective because they were not sufficiently empathic with the parents' desire to hold on to their grown children. This empathic deficiency often is the result of a more general inability to imagine what motivates behavior we find difficult to understand.

The unwillingness of parents to let sons and daughters leave is prompted by a variety of emotions and principles. Parents dread abandonment. They hold on to their children out of the fear that if they let them go, they will never return. Children have roles, sometimes hidden even to the parents, that are essential to the stability of a parent or a marriage or a family system as a whole. It is not clear, for instance, how Mark's irresponsible behavior stabilized the Peterson family system. In families like the Fogertys, the rules about when and how things are to happen lend stability to cycles of life. When and how to leave home is simply a matter of principle: children are at home until they get married and have their own home.

Empathy itself does not change things. It will, however, confirm parental integrity. It may also lessen unnecessary hostility that is directed at the child who is leaving. Most parents intend only the best for their children. Staying at home— or at least close to home—is understood to make life better for everybody but most of all for the son or daughter. The shame that the Fogertys felt because of Daniel's "premature" departure was not feigned. Their parental responsibility to care for their children until marriage had been disrupted. Some of their anger was because this principle had been violated. It would have helped if Daniel could have acknowledged that.

Pastoral work that intends to enhance the process of leaving usually includes something like guidance in addition to support and occasional advocacy. The manner and means of leaving home need to be governed by values that honor community and belonging, as well as autonomy. When viewed from the perspective of cultures that give primacy to the family living within a larger social context, leaving itself is an ethically complex action. There may in fact be ethical as well as emotional and financial reasons why a son or daughter leave home later in life. We need to be careful about prematurely labeling a decision to remain at home as a sign of emotional stuckness.

The pastoral task is to support alternative ways of responding to parents that will empower an adult son or daughter to exercise appropriate freedom from parental expectations in order to claim greater autonomy of thought and action. Because pastoral ministry is often with the parents who are being left as well as the daughters and sons who are leaving, it is necessary to be able to balance advocacy with empathy for the losses families experience when children leave home. Balancing advocacy and empathy in pastoral work with families around the leaving home process is as difficult as it is necessary.

Enhancing Change

There are limits to pastoral intervention on behalf of family change. Some of those limits are determined by the lack of specific therapeutic competence for working with seriously troubled families. Moreover, there is not time to respond to all the families that need help. We have noted already that the pastoral access to people in ordinary family circumstances is an asset in assisting with the leaving home process. If coaching children leaving or consulting with parents who have not let go is not enough, then the task of empowering change for the sake of greater autonomy may require intensive psychotherapy. All of these strategies promote necessary and constructive change in situations where change is feared or resisted.

If you don't love the world as it is, you can't change it.
People are reluctant to change under the pressure of conditional
acceptance. Children who struggle to leave or parents who are
unwilling to let go are more likely to change if they believe
they are understood and loved as they are. Conditional parental
blessings do not liberate. Children who contend they are not
free to leave home until their parents change are likely to stay
stuck. Pastoral ministry in such situations must be empathic in
order to increase understanding for the sake of freedom. We
also need to be sensitive to the fear of change that keeps people
mired in a misery that they themselves regard as intolerable.

Every family has an operational belief about change.
Families come to believe what they do about change because of
their history of loss. When a family is unable to let daughters
and sons leave, it is often because the family feels there has already been too much loss. Or it may be that the family's history
is full of secret grief. Or the family may believe that the only
way to keep things stable is to keep things the same. Or it may
be that the juxtaposition of the birth of a child and the death of
a grandparent creates special difficulties.[4] In order to minimize
loss and keep grief hidden, a family may come to believe that
change of any kind is to be avoided. If a family only associates
chaos and grief with change, then it will do all it can to keep
everyone close and everything the same.

"Small change makes large change." This cryptic principle is based on the idea from family systems theory that everything is related to everything else. If that is true, and we believe
it is, then a small change that is real will have a large effect on
the way the family system as a whole functions. It is not necessary—or possible—to realign everything at once. A small,
achievable change is much more important. It is easier to con-
vince people of this need once they begin to understand the
enormous power of families to keep things the same.

If, for example, a young couple in graduate school feels trapped because they have to stay home every Sunday afternoon to receive phone calls from their parents, they could quickly come to resent that contact because it is unnecessarily confining. Telephone answering machines are not enough for parents who need to find their children waiting at the other end. It is a small change for those newly married children to suggest that they would prefer to telephone when it is convenient. Even though they may continue to call on Sunday afternoon, the timing of the call is in their power. The result of that small change is that parents no longer determine who is free to take initiative or whose time is valuable or when parents and children should talk together.

Leaving home is a process with many small steps. Coaching someone who is working at the task of differentiating will be most effective if one is able to insist that small change makes for large gain. Accomplishing achievable goals is empowering because it encourages one to take another step. Small changes that work are a way out of the discouraging belief that nothing one can do will make a difference in the family's way of living.

The change that changes the family as a system will last. Too often, the solutions that we propose become part of a family's problem because they keep things the same. If a leaver's role as the family troublemaker is simply passed on to a younger sibling, the system does not change. When a son or daughter's leaving does not include new freedom to challenge father's point of view, the rules of the family as a system remain intact: father's word is law. If the leaver is expected to call home at regular intervals, obeying parents is still the norm. The relationship between children and parents has not changed to one of mutuality and equal responsibility. According to family therapists Betty Carter and Monica McGoldrick, "Only when the generations can shift their status relations and reconnect in a new way can the family move on developmentally."[5]

Ordinarily, the change that changes things breaks a rule of the system. Father is not always right. Staying in touch is the responsibility of both parents and children. Difference does not always lead to conflict and hurt feelings. It is possible to tell grandma about the abortion because the family pattern of keeping secrets is no longer in effect. Pastoral ministers are sometimes at a disadvantage regarding systemic change because they are expected to promote keeping rules rather than breaking them. Precisely because of that expectation, however, carefully given encouragement from a pastoral minister to put aside a family injunction or reject a family role may impact the system significantly.

In order to enhance the possibility of change within a family system, it is necessary for the helper to be "in" but not "of" the system. Sometimes it is enough for a family to have someone who is outside the system—and who will remain on the outside—listen to a conversation or be present when a decision is made. The presence of an outsider may be enough to change the family's ordinary way of functioning so that something new can occur. If, however, the helper is co-opted by the system, it is likely that nothing will change. The freedom to coach someone leaving home depends on the helper remaining differentiated from the claims of the system. That requires considerable discipline when one ministers to the family being left as well as the leaver. Staying close to the family without being caught in its emotional web is being an empathic advocate.

Insight helps, but it does not guarantee change. This last principle challenges the long-standing assumption that insight is the goal of pastoral work because it precedes change. It may. However, it is also possible to work towards effecting a change in family living as a prelude to insight. Unless people are able to act differently towards their families of origin in the interest of individuation, everything is likely to stay the same. Insight alone is usually not enough to overcome the resistance to change that the family as a system presents.

Even when adult children are aware of the pain and anguish in their lives because they have not individuated, their resistance to change is deep and pervasive. The risk of doing something that would break a family rule or might jeopardize the conditional affection of their parents evokes terror. Sons and daughters are willing to take the monumental risks that they perceive are required to leave home when the emotional pain in their present lives of work and play and intimacy is greater than their fears of an individuated future life. Frequently, these fears have been reaffirmed by messages from parents about leaving too soon or going too far.

Coping Constructively with Change

The effectiveness of the leaving home process depends on how well a family copes with change. There is always a crisis or turning point when important changes occur either for individuals or for human systems. Things either get better or worse. If a child's leaving home generates more change than the system can bear, the family is likely to be immobilized or stuck because it is overwhelmed with the anticipated loss, or it may attempt to minimize the change in order to reduce the tension. If however the process of leaving home happens in a constructive way, the following actions are likely to be present.

Notice the change. The departure of a son or daughter from home will make a difference for the family. Failure to notice and acknowledge change establishes a pattern of pretense that forces grief underground, discourages straightforward communication in the family, and dishonors the diversity that change creates. A family that is able to provide freedom and support for change among its members is likely to honor the diversity that usually follows that change.

There are two parts to noticing change. First, change

needs to be recognized as it is happening. Things will not be the same in the family after one of its members leaves. While that may be the occasion for some celebration, it is still a loss for which everyone grieves a little. It is appropriate for a family to note with sadness that "this will be the last family pinochle game for a while" because the regular fourth is off to college.

The second part of this process is to note the consequences of this change for the family and begin to make the necessary adjustments to acknowledge the loss. When Herbert's son left for college, the family acknowledged his departure with an appropriate celebrative ritual. The family did not, however, note that his departure left a functional system of three. In order to avoid the sadness, the family ignored the change.

Grieve the loss. All change involves loss, and where there is loss, there is grief. If a family is able to grieve, it is more able to adapt to change. The freedom to grieve allows the family as a whole to be sad and to express that sadness in ways that are acknowledged and supported by others.

Every family has a history of loss and a legacy of grieving. A particular family's inability to grieve may be several generations old. Because of the shame connected with grandma's illegitimate birth, uncle's suicide or some other event, a family may mute all sadness in order to continue to keep the secret grief buried. The process of leaving home may also be impeded because it is one loss too many.

Looking at baby pictures and reminiscing about childhood when a daughter or son leaves home is a way of remembering that is an essential part of grieving. To grieve freely about the past opens the possibility of the future. It allows a family to be sad about what is being lost so that it can later focus its energy on adapting to change for the sake of the future.

Take the adventure. Change is not just loss. For the leaver, it is certainly an adventure that opens to a new way of being, new places, challenging opportunities, and the possibility of a new role in the family. The family being left may not experience their daughter's departure for a year in Peru as adventure because they are more aware of the loss. All of us need courage to bear surprises. The family is no exception. Redefining the family may not be as exciting as living in Peru but it may take as much courage, especially if the system will need to make major changes.

It is an act of faith to accept the adventures God sends, with the assurance that God will accompany us into an unknown, uncertain future. It is not change as such that separates us from God. It is our inability to believe that nothing, not our leaving or even our children leaving home, can separate us from the love of God. That promise provides a grounding for families that intend to stay together by changing together. The capacity to change—which makes constructive leaving home possible—is sustained in the confidence that all of creation, including the family, finds its continuity in God's constant re-creation. With this sense of God's presence as a horizon, we turn finally to a consideration of leaving home as a religious task.

6

LEAVING HOME
AS A RELIGIOUS ACT

LEAVING HOME is not an end in itself. It always has
another purpose: to enable us to marry and form a
new family; to allow us the freedom to live and love in response to our gifts rather than to the expectations of others; to
encourage us to "take the adventure that is sent us." Even the
goal of making one's own decisions or making one's own way
is only penultimate. The development of the power to make
and carry out one's own decisions is a preparation for service
that may lead to sacrifice. This concept introduces the theological implications of leaving home.

Three ways of thinking about leaving home link it to the
resources of the Christian tradition:

> —Leaving home is a *religious act* because it implies transcen-
> dence. It presumes that we are open to the new thing that God is
> doing in our lives.
> —Leaving home is an *ethical act* because it implies discipleship or
> vocation. It enables us to discover, foster, and utilize our particular
> gifts for ends beyond the meeting of our own particular needs.
> —Leaving home is a *sacramental act* because it implies reconcilia-
> tion. We leave home so we can go home again. The freedom to go
> back depends in turn upon the promise of forgiveness and the pos-
> sibility of reconciliation and reunion.

Leaving Home: A Religious Act

> Now the Lord said to Abram, "Go from your country and
> your kindred and your father's house to the land that I will
> show you. . . . So Abram went, as the Lord had told him; and
> Lot went with him.   (Gen. 12:1,4)

The story of Israel—and our Christian story—begins with
a leaving home event. That is not surprising, since leaving home
usually marks the beginning of something new. From the account of the death of Abram's father in Genesis 11, one can assume that Abram had not lived long in Haran. It was not his birth
home; he had come to Haran from Ur, on the other end of the
Fertile Crescent. After his father died, there may have been very
little to keep Abram in Haran. Even if God had not called him to
go elsewhere, it might have been a good time for him to leave.

Abram's journey toward an unknown future has been interpreted widely as a paradigm of faithful obedience. He was
willing to follow the call of God to go into a strange land. This
took an act of faith and an act of courage. As scripture reports
it, Abram knew only that he would go to a land God would
show him. This element of adventure and risk is a common
characteristic of the process of leaving home. What makes
Abram's leaving home a religious act is that he understood his
journey as a response to God.

Leaving behind what is familiar or safe is often painful
and difficult. It is never easy to let go of what we have or the
places where we are known and loved. The ordinary and even
necessary process of leaving behind what we cherish is not, necessarily, an inherently religious act. However, when we risk
something new, when we are willing to follow God into an uncertain future, then leaving home implies transcendence. If we
believe that it is God who is doing a new thing, then the journey
"from your country and your kindred" is an act of faith.

Change is in the nature of things. It is the nature of God to change as well. Whatever lives, changes. To be on God's side, therefore, is to be on the side of change. The process of leaving home is a major change for the leaver and the family being left. When we say that leaving home is a religious act, we mean that our willingness to participate in the changes that such a process brings about implies a recognition, however covert or implicit, that we understand what we are doing as a response to God's intent for our living.

Leaving home is also a religious act when it is understood as a response to a call from God. We may believe that God has called us, like Abram, to go somewhere or do something. The call may be understood in terms of our being compelled to take a particular course of action because of what we see of the world's needs. But that is only one possibility; the call that makes it necessary for us to leave home may be the result of discerning our own unique gifts, which we need to develop. By using the language of calling, we are emphasizing that leaving home is not for its own sake. It is our response to God, who invites us to go somewhere or do something or be someone.

> We were a family of five: Mom, Dad, oldest girl (me) and two younger brothers. However, we were rarely just this small group. When I was seven, my youngest aunt came to live with us. She was six years my senior and had been orphaned when she was two. This was my mother's family. My dad had two brothers, one of whom remained a bachelor all his life. For a lot of the time he, too, lived with us. During much of my growing up years, my dad was an alcoholic. When he was sober, he was great. When he had been drinking, it often fell to me to make sure he went to work.
>
> We had sufficient freedom to develop our individual selves and to take on plenty of responsibilities. I felt valued and esteemed by my parents. Any restrictiveness I felt was probably the same felt by most children growing up. I could go

places and set my own study times. I was never thwarted
emotionally or intellectually. In contrast to many of my
friends, I have always believed that I had freedom to grow. I
feel that both my parents were more normal than not, more
generous than selfish, more understanding than domineering.

My actual physical departure from home was not difficult for
me at the time. I left when I was nineteen years old, having
lived at home while I was attending college. I left home to
enter religious life. My mother accepted my decision; my father did not. He didn't overtly oppose it, however. Even so,
my leaving was not made easy. Although we were not an especially close-knit family, I still missed my brothers and parents. However, I was not tied to my family. I have always felt
free to live at a distance: Nevada, Latin America, Singapore.
I have felt free to do and be what I have done and become.

(Donna)

When Donna left home to pursue the "call" to religious
life, she followed a relatively straightforward extension of her
earlier freedom. Leaving when she did may have been
prompted in part by a desire to gain some emotional distance
from an alcoholic father. She sees it as "free to go." Sometimes, however, the relationship between this sense of God's
calling us—or a feeling that we are invited to "take the adventure that is sent us"—and the ordinary and necessary process of
leaving father and mother is more complex.

Donna may not have had as much freedom as she
thought, since adult children of alcoholics often feel impelled
to make career choices that will take them far from their families of origin but in such a way that they can "blame" their career for the separation. The call becomes a way out of a family
that is stuck. We may also use the claims of our originating
family to resist the call of God. Or we may use our understanding of God's call to circumvent the sometimes painful process
of leaving home.

Understanding Vocation in Everyday Life

This approach to leaving home as a religious issue rests on the familiar theological concept of vocation or calling. We understand "vocation" as meaning the sense of being called, of making life choices—work, marriage, childbearing and child-rearing, parenting, citizenship, even recreation—in response to what one understands to be God's will for one's life. We intend to use vocation in this broad sense to mean the same as ministry in daily life. Vocation is our calling: ministry is what we do in response to that call.[1]

In some religious traditions, vocation is used in a limited sense to refer to the call to full-time ministry in the employ of the church. At most, we often think, people are called to some form of professional life: medicine, teaching, law, and the like. We are less likely to think about parenting or being a spouse as a vocation. It is also held that those who have this special calling received it in the course of some dramatic, personal religious experience. The "call in the night," such as that of the boy Samuel (1 Sam. 3), is taken as the model.

Each individual's calling is a gift from God. In baptism, we are called into the ongoing creativity of God. By providence, we are given gifts that channel that creativity into particular, individual forms. That is our second calling. Our understanding of vocation is that all Christians are given those two calls. Some Christians may also be called by the church, but such a call is not necessary for Christian vocation.

The Family: Where We Are First Called to Ministry

The family is the primary context in which people are individuated. From a religious perspective, it is also where we are trained and called for discipleship. It is a place of criticism and care in which we discover the gifts we have to offer, and where we develop the courage we need to use those gifts for the sake of God and the world. Mothers and fathers who understand their vocation of parenting in relation to God's call will love their children and then let them go. We cannot keep them for ourselves. We nurture them and then let them go because we know they do not belong to us, but to God.

A family's willingness to release the children it has protected and nurtured from the beginning of life is an expression of confidence in their maturity. It is also an act of faith in the providential care of God. Sometimes parents have a difficult time letting children go because they are concerned about their safety or general well-being. Or parents hold on to their children because they do not believe anyone will care for them as well as they do. If our parenting is informed by faith in God, however, then it is easier to let children go because we believe that God continues to watch over them when we no longer can.

The experiences that we have in the family also influence the selection of our vocation and the expression of our ministry in particular ways. Families foster individual gifts but they also assign particular roles. The roles that we came to fulfill in our families of origin are often subsequently reflected in the work we feel called to do. The family helper or responsible child or healer or peacemaker or moralist is likely to select a ministry in adulthood that will continue a familiar role. Continuing that role is one way of understanding how our first call from God may indeed occur within the context of our family of origin.

Our ministry may also be a continuation of expectations or obligations from our families of origin. Sometimes we have been promised to God (as Hannah promised Samuel) out of the gratitude of a parent or as part of a bargain for recovery from sickness. When Kenneth was three, he had pneumonia. His mother promised her only child to God if God would heal him. She did not tell Kenneth of this promise until he began seminary. Sometimes children receive a mantle to do something special—not unlike Joseph's coat of many colors—by being given grandmother's rosary or Uncle John's theology books or being told the secrets of the family by Aunt Emma. With the "mantle" comes a blessing and an expectation that the recipient will do something quite special in the world.

Responding to God's Call

We may think about our ministry as a continuation of family roles or patterns in other ways. Our particular ministry may be to pay a debt for having saved a parent from depression or having kept parents from divorcing. It may be that long before we could say yes or no our family selected us to be its gift to the world or its sacrifice to God. It is important for the sake of our vocation to understand this continuity with our first call. At the same time, we need to make those early promises or obligations our own. That is one way in which leaving home becomes a religious act.

If our response to God's call is why we leave home, it is still essential that we work through the process outlined in the previous chapters. If we do not, then there is a danger that we have used the religious perspective to effect an emotional cutoff that only gives the appearance of leaving home. What is particularly significant about emotional cutoff is that those who engage in it are still powerfully tied to their families of origin even when they think they are following God. If they were not so bound, they would not need the defense of emotional cutoff. We are actually not free from the home of origin nor are we fully free to follow a call if we spend our days looking over our shoulders to be sure we are still cut off from family claims.

From a religious perspective, the goal of leaving home is partnership with God in the ongoing work of creation. Insofar as the process of leaving expands and establishes the formation of a self related to but no longer subject to the claims of our family of origin, it is the prerequisite for discipleship. Our change in status within our family of origin permits us to put other claims—including God's—in a different perspective. If we have become friends with our parents, it will be easier to understand our vocation in the light of these words of Jesus to his disciples: "I do not call you servants any longer, because the servant does not know what the master is doing; but I have called you friends, because I have made known to you everything that I have heard from my Father" (John 15:15). The more complete our sense of being an autonomous self, the more we are able to attend to the nature of the gifts we have been given and to the needs of the world. We are then less likely to accept others' definition of us and less subject to the often exclusive claim our families of origin want to have upon us.

Leaving Home: An Ethical Act

> Then his mother and his brothers came; and standing outside, they sent to him and called him. A crowd was sitting around him, and they said to him, "Your mother and your brothers and sisters are outside, asking for you." And he replied, "Who are my mother and my brothers?" And looking at those who sat around him, he said, "Here are my mother and my brothers! Whoever does the will of God is my brother and sister and mother." (Mark 3:31–35)

Among the sayings of Jesus we find some hard words about the obligations of discipleship. We are to give up our possessions or let go of self or be willing to let the dead bury the dead. Each passage is a test of fidelity and trust. It challenges all prior claims on our lives. In each circumstance, Jesus seems interested in knowing whether or not the call of God claims our highest allegiance. The frequency with which the question is asked about family in one way or another is an indication that the claims of our origins have enormous power.

The chapter in Mark that concludes with Jesus' words about the limits of family loyalty begins with the call of the

Twelve. Jesus called James, John, Andrew, and Peter away from their homes, families, and dependable work and to discipleship. Leaving home is an ethical act when it includes a commitment to a vision or a dream. Such visions and dreams often involve an intent to serve the human community in some way, but that is not the factor which makes following them an ethical act. It is an ethical act when the impetus to leave father and mother is not merely personal freedom or psychological growth but a response to what in theological language is referred to as a *call*.

There is an intricate, intimate relationship between the ethical idealism of leaving home to serve the world and the growth of self and personal freedom that comes from leaving home to make use of the unique personal gifts one possesses. The first has to do with vocation, and the second has to do with "providence." Leaving home is an ethical act when it brings these two strands together, when we understand that we are using the gifts that we have nurtured for service in the world for God's sake. Such discipleship challenges our familiar allegiances and comfortable expectations, some of which have come from our families of origin.

Because the claims of our originating families are often so strong, it is difficult to cut the ties without feeling guilty. Even if our actual families let us go, we may have internalized images of fathers and mothers that impede our freedom either to honor our providential gifts on the one hand or to follow what we perceive to be God's call in this or that concrete situation on the other. Leaving home is made easier if we can relativize the claims of our family. The sayings of Jesus about the family can assist us with that task. We owe our families our gratitude but not our souls. We fulfill our obligation to honor our parents through a service in the world that may take us far from our origins.

The testimony of scripture is that the family is a human

necessity but not the final aim of human existence. Despite the radical nature of his sayings, Jesus does not call for the dissolution of the family; he simply limits its significance. In commenting on Mark 3:31–35, Paul Tillich insists that family relations or obligations are conditional. The words of Jesus about even "hating" father and mother "cut with divine power through the natural relation between members of the family whenever these relations claim to be ultimates."[2] Families may generate guilt when we leave them, but they cannot claim our absolute allegiance. It is the community of those who seek to do the will of God that demands our unconditional loyalty.

There is something both familiar and poignant about the family crisis described in the third chapter of Mark. Jesus' family had not seen or heard what Jesus had seen and heard in his call to ministry. Without understanding that vision, they could not make sense of his extraordinary behavior. His family wanted to take him home because it seemed to them—from their limited perspective—that Jesus had lost his bearings. It is particularly painful when our own families do not see what we see or understand the call that takes us from them.

> Carlisle came from a middle-class family in the South. His father had worked very hard for what he had achieved and had instilled the same drive for excellence and success in his two children. When he entered college, Carlisle was not sure what kind of work he wanted to prepare for. Eventually he settled on law school and finished at the top of his class. He was very successful in his first position, but after about three years it felt hollow. He was not able to find meaning in making wealthy people more wealthy. He left the law firm and the Episcopal Church to live and work at the Catholic Worker House as an advocate for the poor. Even after six years in that setting, his parents still question the wisdom of his decision because they have not seen what he has seen or heard what calls him. They cannot bless what they cannot understand.

It is tragic when our families hate us or label us crazy because our visions do not fit their dreams for our future. It seems very clear to the parents of Carlisle that he has lost his bearings. Under those circumstances, the saying of Jesus seems less harsh and more understandable: "Whoever does the will of God becomes my brother and sister and mother." Those who share a common vision have a common bond that helps overcome the pain of being misunderstood. We can never be without community. The end of the process of leaving home is to discover and be sustained by new contexts of belonging.

The Family as Sending Community

Leaving home to obey a religious call or to follow an ethical vision is easier if the family understands itself as a "sending" community. The family (as we will explore in a later volume in this series) needs to be a "holding" environment in which hospitality, justice, compassion, and forgiveness prevail. But it is also a sending environment; from a Christian perspective, the family is never an end in itself.

Understanding the family as a sending community is in part a matter of survival: it prevents stagnation; it limits excessive privatization; it challenges the covert belief system of most families that nothing bonds like blood. The family is a sending community because the obligations of discipleship transcend the many social and individual needs that the family fulfills. The family is the context in which we discover our gifts in such a way that we can give them away. We are held in order to be sent.

It is not easy for a family to be a sending community. We are ambivalent about our children's maturing. Parents want their children to grow up—but not too big—and go away—but not too far.[3] Even though we may have known from the beginning that our children are not "our" children, letting them go is still painful. For Christian parents, infant baptism or child dedication is an early warning. It is a reminder that our child belongs to God and to the world that is in God's care. We send our children because we cannot keep them.

Some families may have found ways to ritualize sending a child into the world by means of a special meal or a family gathering or a gift that honors the unique attributes of the one leaving and celebrates the life that has been chosen. Other families may resist the choice as a way of holding on.

> When Larry Smith told his parents that he had volunteered to spend a year as a medical intern working for a human rights organization in Guatemala, he was unprepared for his father's strong emotional reaction. Larry's father was understandably nervous about his son's safety. What the father chose to ignore was that Larry's decision to go to Guatemala was a logical extension of the father's longstanding commitment to peace and justice. The father's fear led him to put obstacles in the way of Larry's leaving.

Families that resist sending their sons and daughters often act out of the parents' dread of abandonment. Parents are reluctant to bless their children and let them go because they are afraid that they will not come home again, even if they come to no harm. Parents may also feel abandoned if their sons and daughters dream dreams or make commitments they do not understand. By the time his family went to Galilee to try to "fetch" him, Jesus had changed so much that they could not cope with what had happened. He was not the same person he had been when he left. He did not fit anymore. He was so different they could only conclude that he was crazy. This dread of abandonment may prompt families to take their children into "protective custody" or hold them hostage emotionally.

Commissioning Those Who Are Sent

When children are reluctant to leave home for an uncertain future and families are reluctant to let them go at all or to send them out with a blessing, it is helpful to remind ourselves that we were called in our baptism to service in the world. Unfortunately, most religious communities have limited their confirmation of that call to those set apart for professional religious leadership. As a result, we have not developed ritual processes by which to commission leavers for their own particular expressions of discipleship. Our understanding of leaving home as an ethical act would be enhanced by ritualizing the movement toward the vocation we believe we are called to follow.

Leaving home is not merely for its own sake. We leave home so that we can go home again. We also leave home so that we are as free as possible to move in the direction we believe God to be calling us. This call, according to Luther, first happens in our baptism. We are forgiven and then sent to serve. For that reason, our service is rooted in forgiveness. Baptism is an invitation to risk and even fail because of the promise of forgiveness. Because of that promise of forgiveness, we are free to act responsibly in the world for the sake of God and neighbor, though we know our response will be imperfect.

When religious groups take up their own responsibilities as "commissioning communities," that commissioning becomes a form of ecclesial call to confirm the church's faith in God's ongoing activity in the world through the life of a particular person. Thus, the church is in a position to put the structural and corporate elements of vocation in place. What is needed, however, is the promise of forgiveness, a ritual of commissioning that would contain the promise of response and support for the efforts of each person preparing to follow the call she or he has received.

> "Ruthie," an only child, had lived in a large Western city all her life. Her father had walked out on the family when she was ten. As a junior high student she became an active member of a medium-sized church. Her mother considered Ruthie a "wonderful child, very talented." Ruthie's home city had a large university, where she got bachelor's and

master's degrees in speech therapy. Mother objected vigorously when Ruthie announced plans to complete a Ph.D. in a distant state, and hinted that her daughter was probably a "professional student" who would never allow herself to finish her education. Ruthie persisted with her plans, but seemed to be carrying a heavy emotional burden.

Her pastor responded to the situation in three ways. First, she suggested that the church have a "farewell time" during worship on her last Sunday in town. Second, she designed that farewell time as a "sending service." Third, she repeatedly used the name "Ruth" instead of "Ruthie" in the service, thinking that perhaps the use of an adult name rather than a diminutive would acknowledge Ruth's growth. Later, Ruth wrote back just after a difficult period in her doctoral program to say that the "sending service" had enabled her to "hang in" during that difficult time.

When the church acts to "commission" or to "send" those who have been baptized into discipleship, such a ritual action enhances the freedom to leave home. At the beginning of life, baptism or dedication is understood by parents as a sign that this child they have been given to care for does not belong to them. As we move into adulthood, we understand baptism as a personal call to action. In the confirmation of this call, we become aware of obligations that transcend familial claims. The new community to which we belong by baptism comprises our sisters and brothers who do the will of God. The ritual of sending kept alive in Ruth's memory a sense of belonging to this sustaining community of believers.

Leaving Home: A Sacramental Act

So he set off and went to his father. But while he was still far off, his father saw him and was filled with compassion; he ran and put his arms around him and kissed him. Then the son said to him: "Father, I have sinned against heaven and before you; I am no longer worthy to be called your son."

> But his father said to his slaves, "Quickly, bring out a
> robe—the best one—and put it on him; put a ring on his fin-
> ger and sandals on his feet. And get the fatted calf and kill it,
> and let us eat and celebrate; for this son of mine was dead
> and is alive again; he was lost and is found!" And they
> began to celebrate.   (Luke 15:20–24)

It has been said that this parable is about a "prodigal son"
or a "waiting father" or sometimes the "son who stayed home
instead." Each of these perspectives elicits a significant dimension of the story. From yet another angle, it is a story about
"going home again." Although the son did not anticipate his father's welcome, he was able to return home because he believed
that his father would treat him as fairly as he treated the servants. Had he not been able to trust the forgiving spirit of his father, the son would have stayed in the far country. When the
promise of forgiveness is not present, we are more likely to stay
away from home—which is not the same as leaving. For that
reason, we are suggesting here that leaving home is a sacramental act because it implies forgiveness and reconciliation.

By suggesting that leaving home is sacramental, we do
not intend to elevate commissioning to the status of sacrament.
We are using sacramentality in a broader sense. Acts of the
church and moments of the Christian life are sacramental
whenever the unconditional promise of God's grace is manifest. Sacramental action also reflects our fidelity to Christ who
first summoned us in our baptism. Leaving home is a sacramental act when it begins in Christ and extends through the
church's life and action in the world.

We have suggested throughout this volume that we leave
home so that we can go home again. We are, of course, different
when we return. But so is home. We have also implied that if we
can go home again, we were free to leave in the first place.
From the limited information in Luke's text, we can only pre-

sume that the son in the parable needed to leave home to find his own way. We do not know whether he left angry. Nor do we know whether he told his older brother that he was leaving. It is clear that he thought he had to leave, for whatever reason. It may have been because his older brother had the corner on virtue and responsibility. Undoubtedly, the father was not happy about his son's request but gave him the inheritance anyway. When the father did not hear from his son, he did what most parents do: he imagined the worst. Because he imagined his son to be dead, the father knew how glad he would be to see him again. The son did not know his father's longings. For the son to go home again, he had to believe that forgiveness was possible.

Of all the human communities in which we participate, the family is the one where we are most known to be sinners. It is hard to hide at home. The "prodigal son" knew that better than his older brother. Since the family is such a difficult place in which to hide our sinfulness, it is a community where forgiveness is both longed for and necessary. We want to be understood and accepted by those whom we love despite our faults and transgressions. Parents need to be able to forgive themselves for the ways in which their sins are mirrored in the behavior of their children. Forgiveness is particularly necessary for family survival because buried anger, unresolved conflicts, and unforgiven violations of intimate trust are so disruptive to the human community. Accumulating grievances and resentments is one sure way to undermine the vitality of family living.

Forgiveness works both ways in families. Children forgive and are forgiven. Parents are forgiven as well as forgiving. Being able to forgive one's parents for just being good enough may be a necessary part of the process of leaving home. Implied in the shift in family status is mutual respect and recognition that children are not always what we wish them to be—and neither are parents. When that mutuality is acknowledged, young adults can appreciate parents as they are, no longer needing to make them into what they are not or blaming them for what they could not be.

It is too easy for families to be labeled dysfunctional by daughters and sons who struggle with the task of emotional separation from their origins. Without forgiveness, resentments are preserved and hostilities are nurtured in ways that keep children emotionally locked into the families of their origin. Without forgiveness, children cut themselves off from parents in such a way that their return is blocked. There are offenses in families, like sexual abuse, that may never be forgiven. And other violations of children by parents may not be easy to pardon. Most families, however, are good enough and most sins in the family are forgivable. Part of leaving home is being able to forgive our parents for not being all that we needed them to be.

The image of home as the place where "when you have to go there they have to take you in" is transformed by the Christian vision of compassion and forgiveness. A family shaped by Christian principles is a place where each one seeks to understand and honor the uniqueness of others. It is a place that will take you in as a matter of justice. It is also a community of compassion and forgiveness. Everyone in a family shares in the others' sin and suffering. We are never alone in our pain, nor are we isolated by our sin. Because the family is a company of sinners, it needs regularly to be transformed by the new order of God's love and forgiveness.

> Arthur and Luellen's five sons grew up in a warm, solid home. It was all the more solid and warm for its firm discipline. Their home was a place of criticism as well as care. Only Wendell, their third son, did not seem to fit. From adolescence he did not seem to share any interests with his parents or with his brothers. Wendell would often leave the house in anger because he felt misunderstood. Nobody was surprised when he left for the West Coast the moment he fin-

ished high school. He seldom wrote; and when he did, the let-
ters were bland. At Christmas, Wendell always came home to
share in the family's traditional celebrations and managed to
be reasonably pleasant to the many guests that showed up.
But there was a wall, and no one ever discussed it.

One August, Wendell sent a letter saying he was coming
home. He arrived the same day the letter did. That evening
at supper, Wendell announced that he had AIDS and had
come home to spend his last days. Within three days he was
hospitalized, and after only a week in the hospital, he died.

Arthur and Luellen spent most of that week at the hospital
with Wendell. Their conversation was rich and deep. The
withdrawn, sullen young man, who had kept a wall up for so
long, acknowledged that fear and loneliness had driven him.
Wendell had idolized his father so much that he could not
bear to tell him that he was gay. Arthur was not much of a
talker, either. He had never said how deeply he loved this
son he did not understand. But all that fell away in the hospital. Communication was no longer sparse, and forgiveness
was plentiful. When Wendell died, his parents were on either side of the bed, holding his hands.

At Arthur and Luellen's request, Wendell's memorial service was a celebration of the last three weeks of his life.
Luellen wrote this statement, read at the service by Cyndi
Beasley, a friend of Wendell's who had known about his ho-
mosexuality since both were sophomores in high school:
"We thought we had lost Wendell many painful years ago.
And it may seem to some of you sad that we should, in a
sense, have now lost him twice. Or perhaps it seems sad that
he returned home just in time to tell us first of his sexual
preference and then that he was dying of AIDS. But before
we lost Wendell the second time, we truly found him. We
shall miss him very much. But we shall also live with the
love he brought home."

Not all gay sons with AIDS can come home to die the
way Wendell did. At some level, he must have known what the

prodigal son knew: that his family was a place of compassion and forgiveness. No situation challenges a family's capacity to be compassionate more than to have a loved one dying of AIDS. The suffering and anguish of that circumstance is often compounded, as it was with Arthur and Luellen, by the simultaneous discovery of a homosexual orientation. Families like theirs, who have become a place of care for the person with AIDS have found an otherwise undiscovered depth of compassion in their lives.

AIDS in the family is not the only situation that calls for compassion. The birth of a severely handicapped child sometimes mandates more affection than parents have to give. A teenager's suicide attempt is so terrifying for everyone that the compassion and forgiveness needed is covered over by retreat and recrimination. When the work that one does is corroded by a dehumanizing environment, it becomes a matter of survival that the family is a compassionate haven. To have a parent or a spouse with Alzheimer's is an awkward and agonizing struggle for others in the family. Each of these situations reminds us that being compassionate with one another in families is not a luxury; it is what we need in order to endure.

It is easier to leave a family that is compassionate and forgiving because we know we can always go home again. To be such a community is to hold the suffering of one another in the memory of Christ, who himself has borne all our sorrows and carried all our griefs. In that memory, the lust for power can be transformed into a longing for intimacy; the impulse to compete is transformed into a passion for understanding; the inclination to hide in our families is transformed into a desire to know and be known even in our weakness. A family whose life is transformed by the way of Jesus lives with this inescapable paradox: The family respects the uniqueness of each of its members, and yet everyone suffers when one member is hurt or in pain.

Conclusion

We began our consideration of the art of leaving home with a reconsideration of the importance of home. Because of changes in our time, finding a home rather than leaving home may be the dominant agenda of the next decades. However, in this society, leaving home still remains a transition in family living that is not always easily accomplished. It is complicated by economic and cultural factors, by the leaver's fear of an uncertain and sometimes foreboding world outside the home, and by the inability of a family to acknowledge and grieve the changes that are occurring as family members grow up and grow older.

Leaving home is not an end in itself. We leave home in order to solidify the formation of an autonomous self. We leave home in order to make a home of our own. We leave home in order to be free to exercise our gifts for the sake of others. And we leave home in order to be free to return to the home of our origins. Looked at from our perspective, leaving home is a religious act because it implies transcendence, it is an ethical act because it invites us to unconditional discipleship, and it is a sacramental act because it implies forgiveness and reconciliation. Each of those perspectives strengthens our resolve to leave home in order to fulfill our vocation to make the world a home.

The family is a human necessity. For that reason, some form of community like the family will be needed as long as humankind endures. Because the human creature is so fragile and vulnerable for so long, we need a protective environment in which to grow. Because the human creature is a communal being, who never outgrows the need for attachment, we will always need a holding environment of some kind in which to love and be loved. Even so, the family is not the final aim of human life. The biblical tradition affirms the family but limits its significance. Discipleship transcends what creatureliness necessitates. Christians take the family seriously, but never with ultimate seriousness, lest it impede our leaving home to follow our call.

NOTES

Introduction

1. Kahlil Gibran, *The Prophet* (New York: Alfred A. Knopf, 1923), 17.

2. We have found the most responsible treatment of the issues of codependency in Claudia Bepko and Jo-Ann Krestan's *Too Good for Her Own Good: Breaking Free from the Burden of Female Responsibility* (New York: Harper-Collins, 1990). The discussion applies to the burdens of male responsibility as well.

3. Herbert Anderson, "The Family as a Context for Change and a Changing Context," in LeRoy Aden and Harold Ellens, *The Church and Pastoral Care* (Grand Rapids: Baker Book House, 1988), 57–68. The most comprehensive treatment of the family life cycle perspective is found in Betty Carter and Monica McGoldrick, *The Changing Family Life Cycle* (New York: Gardner Press, 1988). See also Frank S. Pittman III, *Turning Points: Treating Families in Transition and Crisis* (New York: W. W. Norton & Co., 1987) and Celia Jaes Falicov, ed., *Family Transitions: Continuity and Change Over the Life Cycle* (New York: Guilford Press, 1988).

4. Parker Palmer, *The Promise of Paradox* (Notre Dame, Ind.: Ave Maria Press, 1980), 38.

5. Paradoxical intervention has been a common method of therapeutic intervention in several approaches to family therapy. See Jay Haley's *Problem Solving Therapy* (San Francisco: Jossey-Bass, 1976), and Gerald R. Weeks, ed., *Promoting Change Through Paradoxical Therapy,* rev. ed. (New York: Brunner/Mazel, 1991). For a careful rethinking of the place of paradox in therapy with families, see Camillo Loriedo and Gaspare Vella, *Paradox and the Family System* (New York: Brunner/Mazel, 1992).

6. Kenneth R. Mitchell and Herbert Anderson, *All Our Losses, All Our Griefs* (Philadelphia: Westminster Press, 1983).

7. Herbert Anderson, *The Family and Pastoral Care* (Philadelphia: Fortress Press, 1984).

Chapter 1

1. T. S. Eliot, "Four Quartets," in *The Complete Poems and Plays, 1909–1950* (New York: Harcourt, Brace and Co., 1950). Originally home meant something more than our personal origins. It was at the heart of what was real. To be without a home in some societies not only meant being shelterless, it meant that everything was fragmented. Also, compare John Berger's *And our faces, my heart, brief as photos* (New York: Pantheon Books, 1984).

2. Sharon Daloz Parks, "Home and Pilgrimage: Companion Metaphors for Personal and Social Transformation," *Soundings* 72 (1989): 297–315.

3. Carol Ochs, *Women and Spirituality* (Totowa, N.J.: Rowman & Allanheld, 1983), 118ff.

4. Mary Pellauer, "Dislocation and Relocation," *Christianity and Crisis,* April 6, 1987: 110.

5. Linda Hansen, "Experiencing the World as Home: Reflections on Dorothy's Quest in *The Wizard of Oz,*" *Soundings* 67 (Spring, 1984): 91–102.

6. Parks, "Home and Pilgrimage," 304.

7. Wendell Berry, *Home Economics* (Berkeley: North Point Press, 1987).

8. Peter Berger, Brigitte Berger, and Hansfried Kellner, *The Homeless Mind* (New York: Random House, 1973). One of the most poignant aspects of cultural homelessness is that people do not know where to bury their dead. Funeral homes charge rent to hold the ashes, while families debate where or which place is home.

9. Parks, "Home and Pilgrimage," 312.

10. Linda Weltner, *No Place Like Home: Rooms and Reflections From One Family's Life* (New York: Arbor House Publishing Co., 1988).

11. Nelle Morton, *The Journey Is Home* (Boston: Beacon Press, 1985), xix.

12. *The Complete Poems of Robert Frost, 1949* (New York: Henry Holt, 1949), 53.

13. Ibid.

14. We are indebted to Paul Rorem for suggesting the connection between procession and return and the process of leaving home in order to be at home. He has developed this theme most recently in "Procession and Return in Thomas Aquinas and His Predecessors," *Princeton Seminary Bulletin,* n.s., 13, no. 2 (Summer 1992): 147–163.

15. C. S. Lewis, *The Chronicles of Narnia* Series (New York: Macmillan Children's Books, 1988).

16. Eliot, *Complete Poems and Plays,* 145.

Chapter 2

1. Jay Haley, *Leaving Home: The Therapy of Disturbed Young People* (New York: McGraw-Hill Book Co., 1980).

2. Helm Stierlin, *Separating Parents and Adolescents* (New York: The New York Times Book Co., Quadrangle Press, 1974).

3. Judith Viorst, *Necessary Losses* (New York: Simon & Schuster, 1986), 21–80.

4. The theme of being separate/together in families is developed more fully in Anderson's *The Family and Pastoral Care*, 59–68.

5. Erik H. Erikson, *Identity: Youth and Crisis* (New York: W. W. Norton & Co., 1968).

6. Robert Kegan, *The Emerging Self* (Cambridge, Mass.: Harvard University Press, 1982), 15.

7. Murray Bowen, *Family Therapy in Clinical Practice* (New York: Jason Aronson, Inc., 1978).

8. Carol Gilligan, *In a Different Voice: Psychological Theory and Women's Development* (Cambridge, Mass.: Harvard University Press, 1982), 8. Although Gilligan has been criticized because her original sample was not sufficiently inclusive of racial and class differences, the basic premise that women and men have a different developmental agenda continues to be examined. See Judith V. Jordan, Alexandra G. Kaplan, Jean Baker Miller, Irene T. Stiver, and Janet L. Surrey, *Women's Growth in Connection. Writings from the Stone Center* (New York: Guilford Press, 1991).

9. Gilligan, *In a Different Voice*, 23.

10. Richard A. Shweder, *Thinking Through Cultures* (Cambridge, Mass.: Harvard University Press, 1991), 73ff.

11. Froma Walsh, in *Cultural Perspectives in Family Therapy,* ed. Celia Jaes Falicov (Rockville, Md.: Aspen Systems Corp., 1983), 12. See also Monica McGoldrick, John K. Pearce, and Joseph Giordano, *Ethnicity and Family Therapy* (New York: Guilford Press, 1982).

Chapter 3

1. Robert Bly and others have suggested that men in particular suffer because they have lost ritual transitions from

childhood to adulthood. See *Iron John: A Book About Men* (Reading, Mass.: Addison-Wesley Publishing Co.,1990). Rites of passage are not value neutral, however. Traditional rituals contain expectations of gender identity and the relationships between women and men that would be inappropriate to reproduce in most western cultural contexts. For that reason, rather than replicate old rites of passage we need to be creating new rituals that will enable both women and men to move toward adulthood in ways that foster mutuality.

2. We are indebted to Coleen Smith Slosberg, who is herself a campus minister, for suggesting that college is a rite of passage that follows the three movements identified by Arnold van Gennep in *The Rites of Passage* (Chicago: University of Chicago Press, 1960). Kent D. Beeler uses the image of transition in a different way in *College Transitions: A First-Year Guide for Parents and Students* (Dubuque, Iowa: Kendall/Hunt Publishing Co., 1991).

3. Bowen, "Toward the Differentiation of Self in One's Family of Origin," *Family Therapy in Clinical Practice,* 529–547. Regarding emotional cutoff, Bowen contends that "the person who runs away from his family of origin is as emotionally dependent as the person who never leaves it." Ibid, 382.

4. Ibid.

5. Mitchell and Anderson, *All Our Losses, All Our Griefs,* 35–52.

6. Viorst, *Necessary Losses,* 158.

7. Harriet Goldhor Lerner, *The Dance of Intimacy* (New York: Harper & Row, 1989). This is a cogent and readable discussion of the long-term consequences of continuing to fulfill family roles after we have left home.

Chapter 4

1. Lynn Hoffman, *Foundations of Family Therapy: A*

Conceptual Framework for Systems Change (New York: Basic Books, 1981), 158.

2. C. S. Lewis, *The Silver Chair* (New York: Macmillan Publishing Co., Collier Books, 1973), 168.

3. Norman L. Paul, "The Use of Empathy in the Resolution of Grief," *Perspectives in Biology and Medicine* (Autumn 1967). For a fuller clinical development of this theme, see Norman L. Paul and Betty Byfield Paul, *A Marital Puzzle* (New York: W. W. Norton & Co., 1975).

4. Haley, *Leaving Home,* 26 ff.

5. Stierlin, *Separating Parents and Adolescents,* 166 ff.

6. Ellen Goodman, *The Boston Globe,* Tuesday, September 16, 1986.

7. Tom James McFarlane, "The Father-Son Relationship: A Correlative Study of a Son's Perceived Paternal Blessing and His Adult Life Satisfaction" (D.Min. research project report, Garrett-Evangelical Theological Seminary, 1988), 2–3.

8. Claus Westermann, *Blessing in the Bible and the Life of the Church,* trans. Keith Crim (Philadelphia: Fortress Press, 1978), 18. Myron Madden in *The Power to Bless* (Nashville: Abingdon Press, 1970) explores the power of blessing to heal in helping relationships.

Chapter 5

1. Chapter 21 in Bowen, *Family Therapy in Clinical Practice.*

2. James L. Framo, *Family of Origin Therapy: An Intergenerational Approach* (New York: Brunner/Mazel, 1992).

3. The family therapist Carl Whitaker has frequently used the metaphor of coach to describe working with families. See especially *Dancing with the Family,* coauthored by William M. Bumberry (New York: Brunner/Mazel, 1988), 58 ff.

4. Froma Walsh and Monica McGoldrick, eds., *Living Beyond Loss: Death in the Family* (New York: W. W. Norton & Co., 1991), 40 ff.

5. Betty Carter and Monica McGoldrick, *The Changing Family Life Cycle,* 14. Michael V. Bloom makes a similar point when he suggests that "the final stage of separation is the development of a new relationship between parent and offspring based on adult/adult interaction." See "Leaving Home: A Family Transition," in Bloom-Feshback & Associates, *The Psychology of Separation and Loss* (San Francisco: Jossey-Bass, 1987), 249.

Chapter 6

1. Words like calling, ministry, and vocation have many theological interpretations. Our approach has been influenced by Luther's vision that baptism is the beginning of our ministry in the church *and* in the world. See "Concerning the Ministry," vol. 40 of *Luther's Works* (Philadelphia: Muhlenberg Press, 1958). The distinctions that H. Richard Niebuhr (*The Purpose of the Church and Its Ministry* [New York: Harper & Brothers, 1956], pp. 64ff.) makes between baptismal, providential, ecclesial, and special call are not as significant for our time as his insistence that we are called to many forms of work, to partnerships with particular people, to being in particular places, and many other kinds of choices that reflect Christian faithfulness.

2. Paul Tillich, *The New Being* (New York: Charles Scribner's Sons, 1955), 106.

3. Howard Halpern, *Cutting Loose: An Adult Guide to Coming to Terms with Your Parents* (New York: Simon & Schuster, 1977). See also Howard Halpern, *No Strings Attached: A Guide to Better Relationships with Your Grown Up Child* (New York: Simon & Schuster, 1979).